media studies

Brenda Downes
and
Steve Miller

media studies

Brenda Downes

and

Steve Miller

TEACH YOURSELF BOOKS

For UK order queries: please contact Bookpoint Ltd, 39 Milton Park, Abingdon, Oxon OX14 4TD. Telephone: (44) 01235 400414, Fax: (44) 01235 400454. Lines are open from 9.00–6.00, Monday to Saturday, with a 24 hour message answering service. Email address: orders@bookpoint.co.uk

For U.S.A. & Canada order queries: please contact NTC/Contemporary Publishing, 4255 West Touhy Avenue, Lincolnwood, Illinois 60646-1975, U.S.A.. Telephone: (847) 679 5500, Fax: (847) 679 2494.

Long renowned as the authoritative source for self-guided learning – with more than 30 million copies sold worldwide – the *Teach Yourself* series includes 200 titles in the fields of languages, crafts, hobbies, sports, and other leisure activities.

British Library Cataloguing in Publication Data
A catalogue record for this title is available from The British Library.

Library of Congress Catalog Card Number: On file

First published in UK 1998 by Hodder Headline Plc, 338 Euston Road, London, NW1 3BH.

First published in US 1998 by NTC/Contemporary Publishing, 4255 West Touhy Avenue, Lincolnwood (Chicago), Illinois 60646 – 1975 U.S.A.

The 'Teach Yourself' name and logo are registered trade marks of Hodder & Stoughton Ltd.

Copyright © 1998 Brenda Downes and Steve Miller

Typeset by Transet Limited, Coventry, England.
Printed in Great Britain for Hodder & Stoughton Educational, a division of Hodder Headline Plc, 338 Euston Road, London NW1 3BH by Cox & Wyman, Reading, Berks.

Impression number   10 9 8 7 6 5 4 3 2
Year   2002 2001 2000 1999

CONTENTS

Acknowledgements

The author and publishers would like to thank the following for permission to use material in this volume:

Reprinted by permission of Fourth Estate Ltd from *The Media Guide 1998*, Steve Peak and Paul Fisher (eds.), © 1997 by Guardian News Service and Steve Peak (page 11); The Mirror (pages 30 and 74); Ethical Wares (page 31); *ABC of Communication Studies*, D Gill and B Adams, Thomas Nelson (page 38); Map symbol © Ordnance Survey (page 38); *Secondary Media Education: A Curriculum Statement*, BFI (page 63); The Independent (page 71); Express Newspapers (page 72); The Daily Mail (page 73); The Sun (page 75); Mixmag (page 77); Penguin (page 80); PA Listings (page 98).

Every effort has been made to obtain permission for all material used. In the absence of any response to enquiries, the author and publishers would like to acknowledge the following for use of their material:

Cassell Softback English Dictionary (page 22); The Times (page 70); Goal (page 78).

1 | INTRODUCTION

What are the media?

There is no precise or agreed definition of the media. John Fiske (*Introduction to Communication Studies*, 1982) divides media into three main groups which he calls presentational, representational and mechanical. He describes presentational media as face, voice or body communication – in other words as communication both verbal and non-verbal in a face-to-face relationship. Representational media exist once they have been created even without further human involvement, so this group includes writing, painting, photography, music composition, architecture and landscape gardening. These media all have their aesthetic conventions and practical techniques; they can record acts of communication (e.g. writing can record speech as a permanent record). Mechanical media, for example radio, television, video, cinema, the press, telephone are used to transmit communication.

Within Media Studies the generally accepted areas of interest include:

- television
- radio
- cinema
- newspapers and magazines
- advertising
- popular music.

Increasingly, new media such as multimedia, CD ROM and the Internet will be involved in Media Studies.

Therefore, in Media Studies we are actually looking at the 'mass media'. This is an institutionalised form of message production and dissemination, operating on a large scale. It involves considerable division of labour in the production process; for example, in television people are involved as producer, director, camera operator, sound recordist, vision mixer, editor, etc. Mass media are therefore the result of industrial activities produced within large organisations.

Why study the media?

In his book *Understanding the Media* (1973) Marshall Mcluhan argued that education is ideally a defence against 'media fall-out'.

F D Rusmone in *The Purposes in Education* (Institute of Cultural Research, 1974) stated 'This new environment formed by the media makes the need for constant criticism, for a continually critical attitude to other people's motives, if you like, much more critical than it has ever been.'

Media are clearly part of our everyday life. In the UK in 1991 the Broadcasters' Audience Research Board (BARB) suggested that children aged 4 to 9 years watched 18.97 hours of television per week, while those aged 10 to 15 years watched 18.83 hours of television per week. During the winter of 1996 the average audience per episode for British soaps was as follows:

> *Coronation Street* 15.6 million
> *EastEnders* 15.8 million
> *The Bill* 10.9 million
> *Emmerdale* 12.3 million

The number watching *Coronation Street* or *EastEnders* was more than 25 per cent of the population of Britain. On 29 December 1996, 24.35 million people in Britain tuned in to watch *Only Fools and Horses* on BBC 1 – the most popular programme in 1996.

Apart from television, we are bombarded by media messages all day long in the form of radio, popular music, posters and printed advertisements, etc.

There are endless debates – Is there too much sex and violence in the media? Are the media too intrusive into people's private lives? Are the media politically biased? Is advertising giving out harmful messages (e.g. the debate in 1997 over tobacco advertising on Formula 1 racing), etc? The media can clearly influence how we view events. Many would argue that the growth in popularity of the Spice Girls has been engineered by careful media manipulation.

If the media have such an influence on us then it is important for us to study the media to understand how they work and influence us.

Media influence

Since the 1940s there has been an explosion in the development of the
media. To put this in context, it is worth thinking about some of the
significant dates in television:

1925	First public demonstration of television – Washington, USA
	First televised moving image – Baird, London
1926	First public demonstration of true television – London
1927	First public demonstration of true television – Washington
1928	First transatlantic television transmission
	First regular television service in UK
	First television recording system – London
1931	First television outside broadcast – London
1932	First known television image to be received aboard an aircraft – Los Angeles
1936	First regular BBC television service
1939	First regular public high definition television in USA
1939–45	Television in UK closed down for reasons of national defence
1941	World's first experimental colour television service – New York
1951	World's first regular commercial colour television service – New York
	First videotape recorder to be publicly demonstrated – Bing Crosby laboratories
1952	Canadian television started
1954	Europe's first television network
1955	Independent television started in UK
1956	Australian television started
	First use of videotape on television – CBS
1965	First transatlantic television programme relay
1967	First public reception of BBC colour television service
1968	First satellite coverage of Olympics – Mexico
1969	Apollo 11 broadcast from the moon
1972	First documentary on portable video equipment televised – San Francisco

1974	First teletext service in the world – Oracle, UK
1976	South African television started
1983	America's first commercial teletext

Sometimes it is difficult to realise that what is now an accepted part of everyday life is a relatively new phenomenon. However, the pace of change will continue with the introduction of digital television which will improve the quality of television reception and increase considerably the number of channels available – in 1998 Chicago had 500 channels available to each home. This will affect our patterns of viewing enormously. Minority viewing will become common – if you are interested in fishing, cookery, dressmaking or stock car racing all will have dedicated channels available to you. Minority viewing has already occurred on satellite and cable with channels such as National Geographic, the Disney Channel, and 24-hour news.

The same change is happening in other mass media. A collection of vinyl records seems prehistoric beside a collection of CDs. Go into any newsagent or drugstore and look at the range of specialist magazines that have appeared in the last few years, made viable by the new technologies of printing and desktop publishing.

As computers become more common in homes, the range of services and information available is going to have a massive influence on the way we live. Already, the Internet and World Wide Web have given us access to information 'at the touch of a button' that would have been impossible to receive a few years ago. CD ROMs are changing the need for print-based media. Why fill your shelves with reference books such as an encyclopedia when you can obtain multimedia information from a disc? In future you will not have to move from the home to access shopping, banking and a whole range of other services – the technology is already available.

Readership of newspapers is steadily declining as we all demand immediate news via the television and radio. A daily newspaper is printed from early the previous evening onwards so the news you read in the morning is already out of date. Only a few years ago news reports from around the world, despite being rushed back on aeroplanes, could easily be days old by the time they were printed. Now satellites can transmit pictures immediately from anywhere on earth.

However, some factors in this progress are worrying. Control of the media is becoming a massive international business. For example, groups such as the Murdoch empire control the media, both print and television, in many countries in the world. The media are now totally worldwide industries – programmes such as *Neighbours* and *The Simpsons* are viewed in more than 80 countries throughout the world.

The characteristics of mass media can be divided as follows, identified by D McQuail in *Towards a Sociology of Mass Communications* (1969):

1 They normally require complex formal organisations.

2 They are directed towards large audiences.

3 They are public – the content is open to all and the distribution is relatively unstructured and informal.

4 Audiences are heterogeneous – of many different kinds in composition – people living under widely different conditions in widely different cultures.

5 The mass media can establish simultaneous contact with a large number of people at a distance from the source and widely separated from one another.

6 The relationship between communicator and the audience is addressed by people known only in their public role as communicator.

7 The audience for mass communications is 'collectively unique to modern society'. It is an 'aggregate of individuals united by a common focus of interest, engaging in an identical form of behaviour, and open to adversion towards common ends', yet the individuals involved, 'all unknown' to each other, have only a restricted amount of interaction, do not orient their actions to each other and are only loosely organised or lacking organisation.

This all seems as relevant today as a definition of media as it was in 1969. Clearly the media influence our lives, both in the developed and in the developing world. It is, therefore, important that we understand the key aspects of the media – how they are organised, how they construct and communicate their messages and how we as audience react to the messages. It is the purpose of this book to provide an introduction to the key aspects of a study of the media.

2 | INSTITUTIONS

Institutions can be recognised by their patterns of behaviour. Therefore, when you switch on the television to watch a programme you normally expect it to start and finish at specific times, and expect it to be a programme of a particular type. There are shared ideas, meanings and practices which illustrate the institutional nature of television. The term institution combines all the aspects of the media, the media producers and their audience and how they react together.

A study of institutions can be divided into the following main headings:

- Ownership
- Control
- Production
- Distribution.

Ownership

Media institutions are involved in the circulation of ideas. This clearly separates them from other commercial companies. Murdock and Golding in their book *For a Political Economy of Mass Communications* (1973) argued that the media are, first and foremost, industrial and commercial organisations which produce and distribute ideas. As companies they must work in a commercial way, i.e. produce a profit for their shareholders. In most cases this profit is dependent on income from advertising. Murdock and Golding identify those forms of development which apply to the media institutions.

- **Differentiation to concentration** – the process whereby a large number of owners is reduced through mergers and acquisitions to a small number. At the start of the twentieth century UK newspaper ownership was dominated by a few powerful press barons, for example, Alfred Harmsworth.

Later this changed to ownership by large corporations. In the UK in 1997, 86 per cent of the newspaper market was in the hands of four companies.

■ **Consolidation and diversification** – companies expand their interest across a broad range of media and other business activities. A good example of this is the expansion of Cable and Wireless into the cable television market by taking over four major cable operations.

■ **Integration** – the process by which companies acquire other media interests through mergers and takeovers.

■ **Internationalisation** – companies extend their interests beyond national boundaries into global markets.

Patterns of ownership vary in countries throughout the world. Many factors will influence the development of ownership patterns. In Britain it is possible to trace the complete history of media ownership as it has developed in both the public and private sectors. The geographical distances between centres of population are very small compared to Canada, the USA or Australia, for example. It has therefore been possible for newspapers and magazines to achieve national distribution. Similarly, with television, public sector television (the BBC) has been produced mostly from the headquarters in London, although with some regionally produced programmes. Independent television in Britain has developed as a series of regional companies but the output has historically been co-ordinated centrally so that most viewers throughout the UK have seen the same output for much of their viewing time.

However, in the UK even this pattern is changing due to integration. As companies merge it is increasingly possible that ultimately there will be only one independent television company.

In Britain the print media are dominated by seven companies:

1 **News International** (35 per cent of the UK newspaper circulation)

UK – *The Sun*, *The Times*, *News of the World* and *Sunday Times*. Owns 40 per cent of BSkyB and News Datacom technology subsidiary.

US – Fox TV network, television stations in many cities, Fox film studio, Fox video, Fox Interactive, New World

Communications Group, FX cable channel, *TV Guide*, *New York Post, Standard Magazine*, Delphi On-line.

Asia – Star TV (by satellite to 54 countries), Star Movies pay channel, half of the Indian Zee TV, AsiaSat2 satellite system, Star Radio, half of Pacific Magazines.

Australia – Half the newspapers sold in Australia including *Herald Sun*, the *Australian Daily Telegraph*, *Mirror*, stakes in TV stations, half of leading air carrier.

2 **Mirror Group** (26 per cent of UK newspaper circulation)

The Mirror, *Sunday Mirror*, *Daily Record* and *People*. Owns 43 per cent of Newspaper Publishing, which runs *The Independent* and *Independent on Sunday*. Owns Live Television and Wire TV and 40 per cent of Scottish Television.

3 **United News and Media** (13 per cent of UK newspaper circulation)

The Express, *Express on Sunday* and *Star*. Owns over 80 local newspapers and Miller Freeman magazines. A £3 billion merger with MAI extended the group's influence into television. MAI owns Anglia TV and Meridian TV and has shares in Yorkshire TV, HTV and Channel 5.

4 **Daily Mail and General Trust** (12 per cent of UK newspaper circulation)

The *Daily Mail* and *Mail on Sunday*. The Trust is the second largest regional paper owner via Northcliffe Newspapers Group. Holdings in Teletext, local radio (through a holding in GWR), Reuters. Owns 20 per cent of Westcountry Television and 100 per cent of Channel One.

5 **The Telegraph** (7 per cent of UK newspaper circulation)

Daily Telegraph and *Sunday Telegraph*.

6 **Guardian Media Group** (3 per cent of UK newspaper circulation)

The Guardian, the *Observer*. GMG owns over 50 local papers and several magazines; 15 per cent of GMTV.

7 **Pearson** (1 per cent of UK newspaper circulation)

The *Financial Times*, owns Longman publishers, and Future Publishing Magazines. Pearson has recently acquired the Grundy Corporation in Australia.

The Rupert Murdoch owned company News International has a dominance in UK newspapers with over one-third of the market, with a major share in UK satellite operation (owning 40 per cent of BSkyB). It controls significant parts of the Asian Satellite TV market and is dominant in newspapers in Australia. Thus this is a good example of the internationalisation of the media.

The recent merger of United News and Media with MAI extended their interest from national and local newspapers and magazines to television, a good example of integration. United News and Media, through the two companies in their magazine division, Benn Business Publishing and Miller Freeman, publish about 120 magazines in Britain and 150 in other countries.

Ownership of local newspapers in Britain is also involved in processes of integration and is dominated by 19 major groups. In the last two years some £15 billion has changed hands in local newspaper deals.

The top ten local paper owners in Britain are:

1 Newsquest Media Group: 175 titles
2 Trinity International Holdings: 120 titles
3 Northcliffe Newspapers Group: 57 titles
4 United Provincial Newspapers: 64 titles
5 Johnson Press: 143 titles
6 Midland Independent Newspapers: 30 titles
7 Guardian Media Group: 100 titles
8 Midlands News Association: 21 titles
9 Eastern Counties Newspaper Group: 42 titles
10 Portsmouth & Sunderland Newspapers: 19 titles.

In magazines, similarly, a few publishers dominate the market. These include:

■ EMAP Business Communications – over 100 titles
■ EMAP Consumer Magazines – nearly 100 titles
■ Reed Elsecker
■ United News and Media – 120 titles
■ Nexus Media.

Television clearly dominates the media consumption in the UK. The government estimate that:

- 97% of all households have a TV set
- 64% have two TV sets
- 28% three or more TV sets
- 40% of leisure time is spent watching TV.

British television broadcasting is divided into three categories:

1 The public sector – the BBC which is paid for by the annual licence fee;
2 The commercial sector – funded by advertisements;
3 Satellite and cable – funded by advertisements and subscriptions.

The public sector

The BBC has an annual budget of which £1,130 million is spent on television and £381 million on radio in 1997. Because of the way the annual licence fee funds the BBC, control of the budget is decided by the British government. In recent years the fee has been tied to the level of inflation. The BBC, in order to increase its revenue, has expanded into more co-productions with companies especially in Australia and the USA and by selling more of its product, for example, through UK Gold on satellite. BBC Cable Services are in the process of coming onstream in the USA.

The commercial sector

The commercial sector in Britain broadcasts on Channels 3, 4 and 5. On Channel 3 (ITV) there are 15 regional licensees plus the GMTV national breakfast station. Channel 3 is the most popular television broadcaster with 1996 viewing figures of 33.1 per cent compared with BBC 1 at 32.1 per cent.

Again, integration has led to fewer owners of the Channel 3 stations. The largest player is Carlton Communications who now owns Carlton Broadcasting (London and the South East), Central Broadcasting (East, West and South Midlands) and Westcountry (South West England). It also has shares in GMTV and British Digital Broadcasting who have gained one of the digital broadcasting licences.

The Granada Group owns Granada TV, the ITV's biggest programme supplier. Granada covers North East England. It also controls London Weekend Television (covering London and the South East at the weekend). They have shares in Yorkshire Television, BSkyB and British Digital Broadcasting.

United News and Media after their merger with MAI owns Anglia TV (covering the East of England), Meridian Broadcasting (covering South and South East England) and also has shares in Yorkshire TV, HTV and Channel 5.

SKY CHANNELS

The basic multi channel package (the channels are asterisked in the listings below) costs £11.99 a month though the main sports and film channels cost extra. A full Sky service costs £26.99 a month with occasional sporting pay-per-view events an additional charge again.

Sky-owned channels

Sky 1*
The most popular Sky channel with "family" accent.
Sky 2*
"Young, aspiring audience."
Sky News*
Hourly bulletins.
Sky Sports 1
Main sports, including live Premiership football.
Sky Sports 2
Extra weekend coverage
Sky Sports 3
Extra extra coverage
Sky Movies
Recent box office hits.
The Movie Channel
Other contemporary movies, mostly from Hollywood
Sky Movies Gold
Old films.
Sky Travel*
Holiday magazine.
Sky Soap*
Soaps old and new
The Computer Channel*
Nerds only

Joint venture

Nickelodeon*
Children's TV.
QVC*
24-hour shopping channel.
The Paramount Channel*
US comedy and drama.
Granada Plus*
Old programmes from Granada and LWT.
Granada Men and Motors*
Hunk TV.
Granada Talk TV*
Chat.
Granada TV High Street*
Consumerism TV
Granada Health and Beauty*
Keep fit and smart.
Granada Food and Wine*
Noshing TV.
Granada Home and Garden*
Advice and "inspiration".
The History Channel*
Documentaries.
Sky Scottish*
"By Scots for Scots".
Playboy TV
Soft porn.

3rd party multi ...

Bravo*
Cult TV and films.
UK Gold*
BBC and Thames oldies.
The Discovery Channel*
Documentaries.
Discovery Home and Leisure*
How-to TV.
Challenge TV*
Games and quizzes.
MTV*
Modern pop.
VH-1*
Wrinkly pop.
CMT*
New American music.
UK Living*
Women's channel.
TCC*
Children.
European Business News*
Backed by Dow Jones.
Sci-Fi Channel*
Movies and series.
CNBC*
24 hour business channel.
Fox Kids Network*
Children.
The Weather Channel*
In July the sun is hot, is it shining? No it's not.
The Disney Channel
... which Sky defines as its "third party premium bonus

If the rules are relaxed further some speculate that eventually there will be only a single ITV company.

Cable and satellite channels

This ITC listing of top cable and satellite channels shows the audience for cabled homes receiving channels available from "satellites or otherwise".

Sky One	2,030,198	Euronews	1,285,599
UK Gold	1,938,059	Christian Channel	1,269,880
Sky News	1,927,147	History Channel	1,210,033
Channel Guide	1,904,314	Sky Soap	1,206,068
Eurosport	1,876,053	Sky Travel	1,206,068
Discovery	1,859,699	Carlton Food	1,129,442
Nickelodeon	1,857,504	Landscape Channel	1,111,757
UK Living	1,852,636	Sky Sports	1,063,296
TCC	1,848,897	Sky Sports 2	1,062,943
Parliamentary Channel	1,848,647	Sky Movies	1,007,639
QVC	1,825,052	Movie Channel	985,916
Discovery (Home/Leisure)	1,815,139	Granada Talk	977,831
TNT/Cartoon Network	1,810,415	Granada High St	938,014
Bravo (Trouble)	1,807,719	Granada Home/Garden ILC	938,014
Live TV	1,775,265	Granada Food/Wine	938,014
MTV Europe	1,772,007	Granada Health/Beauty	938,014
VH-1	1,732,445	Sky Sports 3	932,327
Sci-Fi Channel	1,643,720	EBN	924,593
Travel Channel	1,638,832	Disney	910,467
Performance	1,621,995	Sky Movies Gold	904,819
CNN International	1,608,679	Bloomberg Info	869,945
The Box	1,523,725	Country Music TV	859,767
Carlton Select	1,440,082	Asianet	711,055
Granada Plus	1,351,333	Channel One	575,935
Sky 2	1,339,976	Paramount	572,487
Challenge TV	1,302,506	Weather channel	533,161
Granada Men/Motors	1,293,646	Vision	522,567
NBC	1,288,680	Knowledge TV	113,516
		BET On Jazz	79,473
		Adult Channel	60,919
		HVC	56,233
		Namaste	49,167
		Zee TV	45,184

Satellite and cable

BSkyB dominates British Satellite TV. It is 40 per cent owned by News International and in 7 years has expanded from 5 to 40 channels. It now has over 6 million subscribers (3.5 million via satellite and the remainder through cable). Currently it attracts some 4.3 per cent of the television audience.

At the moment there are some 113 other satellite companies covering subjects such as shopping, business, religion and ethnic broadcast.

Cable television operators claim that some 9 million homes are now accessible via cable with 2.6 million connected. There are 124 stations currently franchised (1997). These are dominated by a few large companies. Cable and Wireless Communication took over Bell Cable Media, Nyex and Videotron. Telewest Communications, Corncast Europe, Cable Tel UK, General Cable and Telecential Communication dominate the cable operators.

These statistics show how the media industry in the UK is dominated by a few large companies. Some cross various types of media while others have specialised in one particular aspect of the media.

In the United States television broadcasting has a more complex pattern than in the United Kingdom. Television is dominated by local television stations who are not themselves the producers of most of the output, but who purchase programmes from national network production companies. These corporate networks are dominated by ABC Incorporated, Columbia Broadcasting Systems (CBS), Fox Television Network, the National Broadcasting Company (NBC) and the Public Broadcasting Service. These five companies distribute to more than 1,500 television stations across the United States. The major cities have stations affiliated to each of these companies, and there may also be local stations which generally broadcast movies and re-runs of older programmes. In addition, satellite services are available throughout the United States.

In 1995, 53 per cent of viewing was of network programmes, 11 per cent independent, 30 per cent basic cable programmes and 6 per cent of pay cable. There are five major cable operators dominating the market in the United States. These are:

■ Tele Communications Inc
■ Time Warner Cable

- Time Warner Entertainment
- Continental CableVision
- Cox Communications.

ACTIVITY 2.1

Starting from a newspaper television schedule, analyse and record the number of production companies whose material is broadcast on one day of your choice.

Once you have a list to start from, you can use this information as the basis of further research into patterns of ownership. As this is constantly changing because of mergers and takeovers, you may wish to choose one company to create your own case study. Use company reports, media yearbooks (available in major libraries) and contact marketing and publicity departments for further information.

Control

Control of the media varies between countries, depending on the legal framework which has been established in each country. The control in some countries is exerted at both national and state levels.

The relationship between ownership and control in Britain is complex. The economics of the company have some effect, for example independent television companies must compete to ensure an audience to attract advertisers. State control is also exercised in various ways. Independent television is produced by companies who must periodically win a franchise from the government.

There are few controls over the ownership of the press. In Britain, anyone can establish a newspaper provided they abide by certain formalities such as printing the publisher's name in every issue. They also have to ensure that they do not fall foul of the laws covering defamation, official secrecy, contempt of court, race relations, etc. There is no statutory ban on the concentration of press ownership into a few hands) If, by merger, the daily circulation exceeds 500,000 the approval of the Department of Trade is required; this may involve a Monopolies and Mergers Commission investigation. However, approval is rarely withheld. The domination of the national press by a few companies is likely to continue due to the high cost of starting new newspapers. Only two national newspapers came into circulation in the 25 years up to 1986. Since then, eight have been launched but only four have survived. In 1991 the Sadler Enquiry estimated that the launch cost of a new daily newspaper would be in the region of £10 million.

Standards in the press in Britain are handled by the Press Complaints Commission (PCC) which was formed in 1991. The PCC has set up a voluntary Code of Practice and advises editors on journalistic ethics. Several issues in the last few years have brought the PCC into focus. Issues of privacy and intrusion have raised questions regarding whether the Code of Practice is a sufficiently strong mechanism to control the press. The death of the Princess of Wales in 1997 highlighted the problems and has resulted in a revision of the Code.

Under the 1990 British Broadcasting Act limits were placed on media mergers. The Act barred cross-media conglomerates from owning large stakes in both the press and broadcasting. Strict rules also existed concerning the ownership of independent broadcasting. This limited the type of person or company which held television or radio broadcasting licences and how many such licences they could hold, and the extent of cross-media ownership by newspapers. Under this Act no one person or company could control more than one national broadcasting licence and no national newspaper could own more than 20 per cent of an ITV company. However, the 1990 Act did not stop the Murdoch empire setting up Sky satellite broadcasting as it was initially broadcast from mainland Europe.

However, the 1996 Broadcasting Act removed most of these controls described above regarding the ownership of the media. The current legislation prevents any one company from serving more than 15 per cent of the national audience. However, it is predicted that these rules will be relaxed.

In television, control is split between the public and private sectors. As the public sector, the BBC is controlled by a Royal Charter and operates under a licence and agreement as granted by the British government. Although the BBC, through its governors, remains independent from the government, some argue at times that the relationship is difficult to maintain. Because the government sets the level of the TV licence and hence controls the income of the BBC, it can perhaps be influenced by government policies.

The BBC produces a list of accepted broadcasting standards in its publication *Producers' Guidelines* (available from libraries and bookshops). This lays out standards relating to bad language, the portrayal of sex and violence, and other matters of taste and decency including the coverage of disasters, racism, sexism and political bias.

The BBC has its own complaints procedure which includes the Programme Complaints Unit and the facility to appeal to the Governors' Complaints Committee. This procedure also covers broadcasts by BBC radio – both national and local.

Independent television is controlled by the Independent Television Commission (ITC). This is the public body responsible for licensing and regulating commercially funded television in and from the UK. This includes Channel 3, Channel 4, Channel 5, public teletext, cable and satellite services. Under the powers derived from the Broadcasting Acts of 1990 and 1996 the ITC:

- ■ licences commercial television services in the UK;
- ■ regulates these services through its licences and codes of practice on programme content, advertising, sponsorship and technical services. There is a range of penalties for failure to comply with them;
- ■ has a duty to ensure that a wide range of television services is available throughout the UK and that, taken as a whole, the services are of high quality and appeal to a variety of tastes and interests;
- ■ has a duty to ensure fair and effective competition in the provision of these services.

(Source: *Factfile*, 1997, ITC)

ITC has a Programme Code concerning taste, decency, the portrayal of violence, privacy and impartiality. Complaints to the ITC are to an independent body with considerable power and are dealt with seriously by the programme companies. The ITC fines companies for breaching the code but in reality the main deterrent is fear of the loss of the licence to operate in a region. In 2002 the ITV licenses are due for renewal. At the time of the last round of renewals in 1993 some companies lost their licences, including Thames TV (covering London) and Southern TV (covering the South), TV am (national breakfast television) and TSW (covering the South West).

In addition for television under the 1996 Act, the Broadcasting Standards Commission (BSC) was established as a statutory body to control standards and fairness in broadcasting. It covers television and radio (including the BBC). As an independent body representing the interests of the consumer, the BSC considers portrayal of violence, sexual conduct and matters of taste and decency. As an alternative to a court of law it provides redress for people who believe they have been unfairly treated or subject to unwarranted infringement of privacy. Its three main tasks are:

1 To produce codes of practice relating to standards and fairness.
2 To consider and adjudicate on complaints.
3 To monitor, research and report on standards and fairness in broadcasting.

The Commission has no powers to compel a broadcaster to apologise or to award financial compensation, although normally a summary of the adjudication is broadcast on the same channel and at a similar time to the programme which was subject to the complaint, together with publishing a notice in local and national newspapers.

The regulating body for independent radio in Britain is the Radio Authority. It fulfils a similar role for radio as does the ITC for television. Film exhibition is controlled by the British Board of Film Censors (BBFC).

The media is therefore overseen by a number of bodies with a range of 'teeth'. Independent Television and radio are quite tightly controlled by the ITC and the Radio Authority, but magazines and newspapers have more freedom. However, the law operates as the ultimate control of the media in the following areas:

Defamation
Defamation is a statement that damages the reputation of an individual or company by exposing them to hatred, contempt, shame or ridicule. This also includes false accusation. Slander is not published defamation; libel is published defamation.

Obscenity
It is illegal to publish material which will tend to deprave or corrupt persons who are likely to read, see or hear it.

Incitement to racial hatred
The 1986 Public Order Act forbids publication of material likely to incite hatred against any racial group.

Blasphemy
Blasphemous libel only applies where a piece of work is 'so scurrilous and

offensive as to pass the limits of decent controversy and to outrage Christian feelings', but under this law only Christians are covered.

Sedition

This bans publication of material which either incites comment or hatred for parliament or the monarch or promotes reforms by violent or otherwise unconstitutional means.

With so many controls it is a wonder so many programmes are still broadcast! However, it is important to remember that any of the above must be proved in a court of law, as McDonalds found in 1997, after a trial lasting 315 days and reputing to have cost £10 million against Helen Steele and Dave Morris. These two published a leaflet in the UK accusing McDonalds of poisoning their customers, cutting down rainforests and employing cheap labour in the Third World. McDonalds won only a partial victory.

The sections above relating to ownership and control raise many issues. How free are the media to express the views of the general public? When you watch the television news or read it in a newspaper, how accurate is the portrayal – how free is it from bias, based on the ownership and control issues?

ACTIVITY 2.2

1 Record the main news of the evening on the principal television channels and examine in detail the items covered. List them in order and time them. You will often find that the main item is different from channel to channel unless a particularly 'hard news' item is available, and the time given and depth of coverage varies. Why?

2 Buy a cross-section of newspapers from the broadsheets to the tabloids and examine their news coverage – why are the front pages and the main stories so often different?

All media coverage has its own slants and biases – some is directly due to editorial control; much of it is related to the interests and views of the audience. Some newspapers have different political leanings.

3 Find out from your library the systems for the control of media output in a country other than the UK. In what ways do these controls differ from the UK pattern of control. For example, is there more, or less central government control?

Production

The production practices of the media have a clear impact on the messages we receive from them.

As stated above, the cost of starting a national newspaper is high and as a result few companies would be in a position to undertake the financial risks involved. The same is true in television.

If you feel that you have an excellent idea for a new programme you can try to contact the relevant programme controller at one of the television stations with your proposal. The chances of success are small indeed. Read the credits at the end of programmes across all the channels and you will soon realise that most programmes are produced by a handful of production companies. Unless you have an established track record in broadcast television it is almost impossible for you to have your programme proposals taken seriously.

Many proposals are for one-off documentaries – the allocations for these are few and far between and it is difficult to gain approval. Proposals for a series are much more favourably viewed. Another major problem for producers is that ideas are often based on programmes that are already being broadcast. A proposal for a similar series would be viewed with less enthusiasm than an original idea.

If you want to submit programme ideas the key is to examine carefully the schedules of the programme supplier you are approaching. Will your idea fit into the types of programmes they are currently broadcasting? Try to identify what programmes they would like to broadcast in the future – a difficult task!

Finance of media production is also a major problem. In Chapter 8 examples are given of the amount of money various outlets will pay for television programmes in the UK. To run a business that makes an economic return in this area is difficult. Only a few large companies achieve this in the short term and many do not succeed in the long term.

However, the media industry is expanding. It is only a few years ago that television in the UK was limited to four major channels and the majority of the programmes for the BBC and ITV companies were made in-house by their own production facilities. Few programmes were made by outside production sources, except for Channel 4. This is now changing. 'Producer's choice' has been introduced at the BBC and about one-quarter of all their programmes are now made by independent producers.

Similarly, independent TV (Channels 3, 4 and 5) have more programmes produced by programme suppliers. Cable and satellite have expanded the market even further. As more channels are available to households an increasing concept of 'narrowcasting' will become more familiar. This is where programmes are produced for specialist or minority audiences.

Who will produce all the extra television that is being demanded and how will they do it economically? As audiences for individual programmes become smaller as a result of more choice, revenue for the programme suppliers will reduce. Income from advertisers will have to be split amongst a wider number of programmes.

The changes in technology will also have impact on the media. In newspapers and magazines new technology has decreased the cost of production so more minority audience publications are now viable. Radio licences have been issued for a wider variety of specialist programmes and more local stations.

In television, cable has had a particular impact. Specialist programmes are now available to minority audiences. The impact of digital technology will have a similar effect on broadcast television. Control of the media will become increasingly difficult, as bodies such as the ITC try to control broadcasts from outside the UK which are received within the country.

The current debate about sport on television raises an interesting question – what rights does the mass audience have to receive major sports events broadcast free on the main channels as opposed to viewing them on subscription satellite and cable stations? Perhaps more events will be available only on pay-TV where a fee is charged for the individual programme, for example as already happens in some boxing contests.

As the technology of programme production changes it also has an impact on programme costs and employment. A few years ago it was usual to see a television news crew out filming with six or more people. More common now is a crew of two or three. A good example of how technological changes are affecting employment is in the main BBC newsroom. Until recently each of the eight cameras was controlled by a camera operator. Now all the cameras are remote controlled by one operator from a central console and, by using a barcode system, much of the operation is pre-programmed into a computer.

Cameras are becoming more lightweight and cheaper. Digital broadcast-quality cameras are now becoming common so that a single operator can use them without difficulty. Similarly, editing is changing. A briefcase-sized digital desk can be carried on to location and used by reporters to edit their own material on site – reducing costs and employment opportunities further.

Distribution

The way in which media texts are distributed is changing rapidly. In television, digital, cable and satellite communications have revolutionised the transmission of programmes and will continue to do so. Fibre-optic cables and enhanced telecom cable with interactive applications will be available to each home. The technology is in place for the information revolution, but is not yet wired to each home. Interactive Broadcasting was launched in 1997 and it is anticipated that 400 channels will be available to homes in the UK. The Internet is predicted to grow from a current level of some 1.5 million homes to 22 million. Armchair services for shopping, banking, holidays and travel, games, learning on-line, entertainment, sports, motor world, e-mail and public services will be available from Interactive Broadcasting. It will ultimately change the way we live – Why send a letter when an e-mail is instant? – Why go to the supermarket or bank when you can do it all from home?

How will these changes affect the audience? In theory, whatever entertainment or information you want will be available to you. Perhaps the days when 10 to 20 million people regularly watch a single programme will be gone forever. What will people talk about when they meet if they do not have not the common experience of watching the same television programme? Playground talk now often focuses on last night's episode of *Neighbours* – in the future that will not be the case as the audience might have watched a wider variety of programmes.

It is difficult to predict how technological advances will change our use of the media. However, it is inevitable that the media will be dominated by large institutions and various aspects of control will be exerted by the governments to try to maintain standards in its media products.

Sources

Information for this chapter on ownership and control in the UK has been drawn from a number of sources.

Four annual publications are of particular value:

1 *The Guardian Media Guide*, **Fourth Estate, London**.

   This gives details of ownership of the national press, local newspapers, magazines, publishers and agencies in the UK. It includes details of circulation figures of all print material.

   Certified circulation details for newspapers and magazines in the UK are produced by the Audit Bureau of Circulation (ABC). The most up-to-date figures are available free on their website on http://www.abc.org.uk.

   The Guardian guide also covers broadcasting – BBC television, Independent Television, satellite, cable and radio in great detail, giving factual information and addresses.

2 *Factfile*, **Independent Television Commission**.

   This free publication from the ITC details the work of the ITC and lists all the licensees including Channels 3, 4 and 5, cable, satellite programme services and cable operators. Current details can be obtained from their website at http://www.itc.co.uk.

3 *BBC Annual Report and Account*.

   This gives an overview of the work of the BBC, both television and radio. It provides details on audience reactions and analyses output.

4 *Film and Television Handbook*, **British Film Institute**.

   This details film production, cinema details, video rental and sales, television trends and awards, and gives many relevant addresses. It has a website at http://www.bfi.org.uk.

All the above will provide up-to-date information.

Relevant information on a weekly basis in the UK can also be obtained from:

> *The Guardian* newspaper (Monday media supplement)
> *The Independent* newspaper (Wednesday media supplement)
> *Broadcast* magazine

For international information it would be useful to consult:

> ■ The *TV and Video Almanac* (United States)
> ■ The *TV International Sourcebook*
> ■ World Television.

3 | IDEOLOGY

Ideology is the word which is most often used to describe a collection of ideas. The third edition of the *Cassell Softback English Dictionary* gives four definitions:

1 A body of ideas that reflects the interests of a nation, political system, etc. and underlies political action.

2 In philosophy and sociology, the set of beliefs by which a group or society orders reality so as to render it intelligible.

3 Speculation that is imaginary or visionary.

4 The study of the nature and origin of ideas.

However, because of the history of the word and the ways in which its meanings have evolved, the term 'ideology' could potentially cause some confusion for the Media Studies' student. It is useful, therefore, to offer a brief overview of these changing definitions and how the term in its current usage can be applied to the study of the media.

Origins

During the late seventeenth century, John Locke (1632–1704) in England and, in the eighteenth century in France, Denis Diderot (1713–1874) and Voltaire (1694–1778) were instrumental in influencing new ways of thinking about the human condition. Previously the ideology of Christianity had dominated European thought, but these new thinkers placed emphasis on rational thought and reason as the only route which would allow humankind to make progress. Rationalist thinkers believed that all people had an equal capacity to reason, that this should guarantee individuals freedom and legal equality and that any reasoned thought or belief should be tolerated by those who were enlightened by this understanding. The rationalists wanted to move away from what they saw as the myths and illusions perpetrated by religion towards a more enlightened approach to life. They believed that individuals should think things out for themselves instead of accepting the authority and ideas of other people.

This period of European history is now known as either the Age of Reason or the Age of Enlightenment. Rationalist thinking coincided with a period of great scientific discovery and invention, and rationalist thought influenced the development of revolutionary ideas about political and social organisation. Historians generally agree that the Age of Enlightenment drew to a close after the French Revolution in 1789, a political change which enshrined the concepts of liberty and equality for all into the organisation of a European country for the first time.

The word 'ideology' was first used in England in 1796 to describe the study of ideas, but is the definition which is used least often today.

The nineteenth century

In his book *Keywords* Raymond Williams traces the history of the term ideology; his research suggests that by the early nineteenth century the word carried a meaning of 'abstract, impractical or fanatical theory', that is, that ideology was seen as grounded in ideas rather than in experience. This links to the third definition of ideology above. The word was used in the sense of an abstract theory by Napoleon Bonaparte to describe those who promoted the idea of democracy as an ideal political system. This use caused the word to become associated with illusion and unreality and led to its use as a negative rather than positive term to describe political and social theories. Some element of this feeling persists in our current use of the word.

Marx and Engels

By the middle of the nineteenth century the meaning of ideology had been developed and expanded upon in the thinking of two German political theorists, Karl Marx (1818–83) and Friedrich Engels (1820–95). Building on the work of European thinkers earlier in the century, for example Georg Hegel (1770–1831), François Fourier (1772–1837) and Saint-Simon (1760–1825), Marx and Engels modernised the concept of ideology. They redefined ideology as the expression of a set of ideas which represented the material interests of particular groups or classes within society. Their work introduced the idea that there could be not one, but many ideologies, each representing the thinking of the different groups which make up society. At any given time, one of these ideologies would be accepted by the majority of the people. This they called the dominant ideology.

Marx and Engels thought that it was the function of the thinkers, or ideologists, within interest groups to create theories which would allow them to promote their own interests above those of other groups. The successful continuation of a dominant ideology relied upon the willingness of a whole society to accept, believe and act upon the common-sense knowledge that the way in which society operated was natural, not constructed by society itself. At the time that Marx and Engels were writing, the dominant ideology in Western Europe was capitalism. Marx and Engels believed that it was the economic organisation of a society which governed every other aspect of the life of its citizens:

> In any epoch the ruling ideas are those of the ruling class, i.e. the class which is the ruling material force is at the same time its ruling intellectual force.
>
> Engels

Since capitalism was the ruling force of the times, it was the ideology of capitalism which Marxists held responsible for the conditions in which people lived. It therefore followed that the only way to improve conditions would be to successfully challenge the dominant ideology of capitalism. This, they believed, could be accomplished only if power was seized from the capitalists, who would not willingly give up their dominant position.

False consciousness

Marxism opened up the intellectual space for people to question the idea that the existing social order was natural. Marx and Engels argued that capitalism was not in the best interests of most of the people who lived within capitalist systems. They thought that the willingness of people to continue living under this system could be explained by their concept of false thought, or false consciousness. Marx and Engels believed that for the dominant ideas to remain so, individuals had to accept that the way in which it defined each of them was necessarily accurate. Marxists did not believe that this acceptance had to be conscious. In fact they believed that for most people the acceptance had to be unconscious for the process to work to the advantage of capitalism. In failing to question the organisation of the societies in which they lived, individuals were accepting a false definition of themselves, which was rooted not in their own need, but in the need of the dominant members of society to maintain their position. Thus, common-sense acceptance could be shown to lead to the adoption of false consciousness.

Marx and Engels believed that there could be different ideologies which could be used as conceptual frameworks by different groups within society. It was, therefore, possible to conceive of a middle class or 'bourgeois ideology' which represented the interests of that class above all others. If society was to change, individuals needed to refuse to accept that the current system of social organisation was natural, and to become aware of the possibility of creating and adopting an ideology appropriate to their own needs. For example, a 'proletarian ideology' would reflect and promote the interests of ordinary working people and offer a framework from which they could think about ways to change their living conditions. By putting into practice the new ideas, different models of social organisation could be achieved, reality could be recognised and false consciousness would be overcome to be replaced by genuine experience. Thus, the thinking of Marx and Engels allows us to think about a range of different ideologies, rather than just one set of ideas.

The twentieth century

A major development in the theory of ideology was built on the ideas of Marx and Engels who saw the dominant ideology as a tool of capitalist oppression of other classes. They believed that only a class-based solution could be sought if the working class was to have the chance to break free from what they defined as oppression.

Hegemony

Following the Russian Revolution in 1918, thinking continued to develop about the nature of ideology. For example Antonio Gramsci (1891–1937) argued that a society's economic system could not be used alone to control every aspect of intellectual, cultural and political life. Gramsci's concept of **hegemony** identified the role of cultural power in the maintenance of the status quo. [Hegemony was defined as the process by which the dominant ideology was able to naturalise aspects of how society is organised and this was achieved through the control of cultural practice.] For example, he believed that newspapers and cinema could be used to promote the viewpoints of the ruling class and the bourgeoisie and these perspectives would be read and accepted by all audiences This concept is related to Marx's idea of false consciousness inasmuch as it recognises the role that the working classes play in their own oppression, but unlike Marx, Gramsci believed that the struggle for change in society could be waged intellectually rather than violently. He believed that change could be brought about through consciousness raising and education and that people would ultimately reject the control of the dominant ideology.

It is possible to spot examples of hegemony in operation in the media by analysing closely the language used to describe current affairs or to represent political issues. References to 'our government' or 'our foreign policy' can be seen as evidence of the inclusive nature of hegemony, which is intended to naturalise and unite the population. The effect on those who disagree with the actions of 'our government' is to set them apart as dissenters: they become seen as 'not one of us'.

The Frankfurt School

During the 1920s at the Institute of Social Research at Frankfurt University in Germany, a group of philosophers and sociologists led by Max Horkheimer (1895–1973) and which included Herbert Marcuse, Theodore Adorno and Walter Benjamin, sought to develop a new Marxist perspective on society and culture. Since these men were Marxists, and some were Jewish, the Institute was moved from Germany to the USA following the rise to power of Adolf Hitler's National Socialist, or Nazi, Party in 1933. They returned to West Germany in 1949.

The theories developed by the Frankfurt School drew on many different disciplines. They developed a theory about the nature of cultural production which treated culture as if it were the same as the output from any other manufacturing industry. They claimed that the function of cultural artefacts was to reflect the interests of the ruling classes both in their content and in the way in which they were produced. Even mass or popular culture was thought to contribute to hegemony because it was seen as a basically commercial enterprise which produced revenue for its producers, not for its consumers. The solution to this problem would be to seize the means of cultural production, not to change only the economic system of production and profit in other industries.

Leavis and Thompson

During the twentieth century there developed, alongside Marxist approaches to the uses of ideology in the media, a second school of thought which took an opposing view. Where the Marxist tradition celebrates the possibility of creating cultural products which function as tools to challenge the dominant ideology, other theorists started from the premise that twentieth-century media expansion has contributed to the destruction of 'real' culture. These theorists saw popular culture as a dangerous and corrupting influence which could be used to challenge the political status quo. The publication of *Culture and Environment* (1933) by F R Leavis and Denys Thompson called for resistance to the popular mass media and a defence of existing cultural values and artefacts.

The idea that earlier forms of entertainment were and are intrinsically more valuable than newer forms is central to the arguments put forward by Leavis and Thompson. This position cannot be separated from their belief that forms such as opera, drama and classical music are properly the province of those who are educated enough to understand them, although others can aspire to this condition. Their position has been attacked as one which promotes elitism and the class system, despite their belief that society may change if individuals choose to overcome their background by using their individual freedom to progress. This echoes the ideas of the Age of Enlightenment.

Eagleton

Terry Eagleton, in his book *Ideology* (1991), discusses the range of uses and meanings which the word 'ideology' has accrued during the twentieth century, and lists the following among current meanings:

1 the process of production of meanings, signs and values in social life
2 a body of ideas characteristic of a particular social group or class
3 ideas which help to legitimise a dominant political power
4 false ideas which help to legitimise a dominant political power
5 systematically distorted communication
6 that which offers a position for a subject
7 forms of thought motivated by social interests
8 identity thinking
9 socially necessary illusion

  10 the conjecture of discourse and power
  11 the medium in which conscious social actors make sense of
          their world
  12 action-oriented sets of beliefs
  13 the confusion of linguistic and phenomenal reality
  14 semiotic closure
  15 the indispensable medium in which individuals live out
          their relations to a social structure
  16 the process whereby social life is converted to a natural reality.

Eagleton notes that:

- not all of the above are compatible with each other;
- some of the formulations are pejorative (i.e. take a negative
  view), some ambiguous, others not pejorative;
- ideology is something that other people have;
- some of the formulations rely on our knowledge of the
  world, others do not;
- some of the above involve a sense of not seeing reality properly.

Ideology in the media

What kind of relationships exist between the media and ideologies?

To answer this question it is necessary to draw together several aspects of
media studies which are discussed elsewhere in this book:

- The media communicate ideas.
- The media represent outside reality to audiences.
- All texts are produced by people.
- All individual producers of texts and media institutions have
  viewpoints.
- No text can exist without offering its consumers a position,
  or 'point of view' to adopt.
- Audiences make meanings and sense from texts in accordance
  with their existing knowledge.
- All media institutions are owned by somebody.

Like many media texts, ideology is constructed to appear to be seamless.
It is sometimes difficult to see exactly how and where the component parts

are joined together, as the development of the narrative diverts the audience's interest away from the ideological construction. Yet it is the construction of the text which can give the media student the best insight into the ideologies which run through texts. For example, choices of how technologies are used to represent race, gender or age, the way characters are lit or shot and the actions which we see them carrying out can all reveal something about the ideology encoded in images. The kind of story, what is included or omitted, and whether the text fits into a particular genre are all the results of choices and these choices contribute to the ideological viewpoints expressed.

Ideological discourse

Some discourses, or areas of discussion, form the major strands of debate in contemporary society. In part, it is the views taken on such issues as these which form the basis of culture and social practice. These issues include:

- equal opportunities
- education
- employment
- feminism
- sexuality
- consumerism
- nationalism/internationalism
- monarchy/republicanism
- racism/anti-racism
- age/youth
- left wing/right wing
- public/personal morality
- crime and punishment.

You will, no doubt, think of other discourses which are of current general, or personal interest. Our personal interest in certain topics influences both what we choose to consume and how we react to it as audience members. The following activities are designed to enable you to analyse how the mainstream media assume that a certain viewpoint may be common among consumers of texts and to offer a structured method of exploring what these attitudes may be.

ACTIVITY 3.1

VOICE OF THE
Mirror
Euro YES
vote will
start here

THE Prime Minister and Chancellor want Britain to be in the European single currency.

But they will let the people decide in a referendum before we go in.

At the moment, the signs are not hopeful of getting a Yes vote. More than half those quizzed in recent opinion polls are against replacing the pound with the Euro.

But before the 1975 referendum on Europe, two in three people were against. Yet when the vote was taken, two in three said Yes.

What made the difference was a fantastic campaign in which all those who realised the value of Britain being in Europe joined. They fought and argued for what they knew was right — and they won.

That is what must happen now. So far, the field has been left to the rabid anti-Europeans who have loud voices in Parliament and powerful friends in the media.

They have been making the running. Now is the time for all those in business, industry, the City and the media who know Britain needs to be part of the Euro to begin the fightback.

No matter when the referendum is held, the Yes campaign has to start from here. And *The Mirror* will lead it.

A lot of people need persuading. But the case is unbeatable and the British people have too much sense to turn away from a brilliant future in Europe.

Read the newspaper article reproduced above, which is taken from the editorial page of a British tabloid daily newspaper.

1 Make a note of any language which assumes that the reader holds the same attitudes and values as the writer.

2 List the ideological discourses which are referred to either directly or indirectly.

3 Try this activity again with other editorial columns and newspaper stories.

4 Follow a story for a week to see how discourses are developed and how new aspects of issues are incorporated and naturalised.

ACTIVITY 3.2

Look carefully at the advertising image reproduced below and read all the copy

1 List the ideological discourses which are referred to either directly or indirectly.
2 Would it be possible to sell the same product to the same intended audience without referring to the same discourses?
3 Draft your ideas.

ACTIVITY 3.3

Consider the example of a famous sportsperson winning in an important international final.

Immediate news reports are likely to feature photographs of a jubilant athlete and a cheering crowd with the image anchored by the text to discourses of heroism, the overcoming of adverse conditions before emerging as a winner and national values.

The next day, it is discovered that the athlete had taken performance-enhancing drugs during training.

Which discourses might emerge within the news reports which follow?

National identity

One of the most important functions of the dominant ideology of a country is to establish and maintain a national identity which citizens can feel part of. This is important to maintain because it creates a sense of social cohesion, gives people common reference points, may build loyalty and patriotism and can be accessed in times of national crisis. There are many things of which we accept we are a part and that we may feel are part of ourselves. We do not question or even think about some of these things much, because they have been naturalised through ideological processes. Once more, a way to make visible the ideological process is by considering some of the representations which are commonly used to carry out this work.

ACTIVITY 3.4

On the following page are three images of Trafalgar Square in London. Trafalgar Square lies at the northern end of Whitehall, which is the location of many government departments, Horseguard's Parade and the Prime Minister's London residence. To the west of the square is The Mall, which leads directly to Buckingham Palace. On the east side of the square is South Africa House, on the north side is the National Gallery. The square is a major tourist attraction and is famous for its fountains, statues of lions, Nelson's column and the thousands of pigeons which go there to feed.

King George IV

Havelock

Napier

Look carefully at the images on page 33.

1 How does Trafalgar Square contribute to the construction of a national identity for England/Britain?

2 Are all sections of the community represented?

3 What does the absence of representation tell you about the status and perceived role of some groups of citizens in the construction of the English national identity?

4 There is one empty plinth in Trafalgar Square. Whose statue would you place on it if you were to try to ensure that the British concept of national identity is to be broadened by the representations in the square?

ACTIVITY 3.5

To investigate how texts across a range of media support a particular ideology, it is useful to choose on one day to listen to radio news bulletins, watch television news and current affairs programmes and buy all the newspapers.

1 Choose one story and follow it through the day and across the media.

2 Choose several stories and consider how the way in which they are each reported contributes to the maintenance of the dominant ideology. Pay particular attention to the comments and interpretations of events which link known facts.

3 How does the reporting of news and current affairs correspond to what audiences expect to hear?

Alternatives

Some media producers do not offer audiences mainstream, or mass circulated texts or mainstream ideologies. Texts which are constructed to offer a different viewpoint on life and society are often described as alternative, that is alternative to the mainstream. These texts are recognisable by their differences from mainstream texts which may include:

- material not often included in mainstream production;
- using non-mainstream narrative forms;
- using mainstream forms to challenge mainstream ideology;
- encoding alternative or oppositional messages in texts;
- production practices reflecting economic constraints faced by small companies;
- circulation through different distribution systems and specialist outlets;
- often being finely targeted at a small audience segment;
- lack of popular appeal;
- lack of commercial success;
- representations which challenge stereotypes or include groups absent from other texts.

Sometimes an alternative text exceeds expectations and becomes a large-circulation popular text. An example of this is the British magazine *Viz* which after small beginnings as a home-produced comic increased its circulation to one million. As the product increased in popularity the producers were forced to abandon alternative production and distribution methods, and it is a matter of debate whether changes in content following this could be considered to have moved the magazine from the fringe and into the mainstream.

Independence

Most alternative texts are produced by independent companies, that is, organisations which are not part of the overall pattern of ownership and funding which characterises the mainstream media. Independent companies may raise funding from a variety of sources including sales, grants and donations, and on the whole tend to run within much smaller budgets than companies which are subsidiaries of larger organisations.

'Independent' and 'alternative' do not mean the same thing. It is important to remember that not all independent companies produce alternative texts; they may produce texts which reflect mainstream ideologies and which are circulated through mainstream broadcasting companies, cinemas or shops. Any television listings magazine will feature a number of independently made programmes which are broadcast on mainstream stations.

Why is ideology important?

Ideology underpins every political system and therefore underpins the conditions in which media texts are created. The strength of the dominant ideology and the challenges made to it by alternative ideologies are usually regarded as important in media studies because media texts are the visible manifestations of the production and circulation of current ideologies.

4 | MEDIA AND LANGUAGE

The study of media language is concerned with how the mass media are used by producers to communicate messages to the audience. Each medium has developed specific uses of language which are appropriate to the technology, methods of circulation and intended audience for the product. Audiences need to use different skills to decode and understand these combinations of print, image and sound as they are used by each medium.

Most of us are taught to become print literate at school. Our society places such great emphasis on print as the primary form of communication that children are encouraged to start the long and difficult process of learning to read print as early as possible. While learning to read print we also learn many other skills which are associated with reading. For example, we learn to ask and answer questions about what we have read, to discuss the content and construction of what we read and to criticise form and structure. Above all, we learn to write and in doing so we accumulate a deeper knowledge of the structure and uses of language. Writing also allows us to become producers as well as readers of text. We all assume that print literacy is a basic right of all citizens. Those who do not know how to read or write often suffer from social disadvantage and exclusion.

By contrast, many people never have the structured opportunity to become literate in the reading of images. There is an assumption within society as a whole that pictures are something that we can understand instinctively, without the need for any training in how information can be encoded within images and decoded by audiences. This privileging within education of print over other forms of communication reflects society's historical attitudes to the media and to education. Attitudes towards 'high' and 'low' culture are echoed within the school curriculum, where the use of media texts is often restricted to their use as audio-visual aids, and where notions of quality control limit the range of media products made available or sanctioned by teachers. Thus for many young people their consumption of non-print media texts operates in a domestic setting, without the benefits of approaches adopted towards the structured consumption of print texts.

Until quite recently, the same attitude existed towards auditory skills and speech. It was only with the introduction of the National Curriculum in England that a structured developmental programme of teaching the skills of speaking and listening was introduced for all school students.

This chapter will concentrate on how information is encoded in images. As the media cannot give audiences direct experience of reality, media texts communicate ideas about reality by using a system of signs, which stand for or take the place of the outside reality.

Reading signs

The study of signs and sign systems, the way in which they are used to communicate and how we understand them is called **semiology**. The system of decoding the signs used in media texts is broadly based on the work of two people: Ferdinand de Saussure (1857–1913) and Roland Barthes (1915–80).

Saussure was a linguist who was interested in the underlying structure of language and how it was used. He extended his studies from language to literature and even to the structures of different societies.

Barthes was also a structuralist. His original interest was in how signs were used in literature and the theatre and how readers and audiences were able to understand them. Barthes devised a system of classifying signs which revealed the underlying structure of how texts are organised.

> Semiotics is the study of the way people generate meanings from the sign-systems that they use for communication purposes.
>
> *ABC of Communication Studies*, David Gill and Bridget Adams

Some signs are extremely easy to understand because they *look* like the things they stand for, for example:

+   **Church**
         or   **without tower or spire**
         chapel

Other signs do not look like the thing they stand for. These types of signs are said to *symbolise* what they stand for or represent. Take this sign for example:

church

The word 'church' does not look like a church building at all, yet the word has meaning for us. This word symbolises many things and may evoke different things for different readers. You may have thought of a building you have seen, an event which you have attended at a church, or the idea of religion.

All words and some visual symbols communicate ideas about objects, ideas, feelings or events. Therefore *signs* are said to signify the things which they take the place of, or stand for. For example, a cross may *signify* a church, but the idea 'church' may make an individual think of death and funerals. In this case the two things, cross as *signifier* and death as *signified*, together for Barthes form a *sign* which can be read as meaning 'death'.

signifier + signified = sign

The order and context in which signs appear influence the meanings which audiences make from them.

Semiology is the study of how meanings are encoded within signs, and how we, the audience, take meanings and make sense of the information contained in signs. Signs are *polysemic*, that is that they can have more than one meaning. The audience makes sense of signs according to personal knowledge, experience and the context in which the sign occurs. Thus we each, unconsciously, select which of the possible meanings to apply, and read the sign accordingly.

Anchoring meaning

The photograph at the bottom of page 39 is reproduced without a caption. As you look at it you are free to create a context, a narrative and a set of meanings for the information it offers without any interference by the person who produced the image.

However, signs can be **anchored** to a particular meaning which has been selected by the producer of the text. Such anchoring attempts to fix meaning and to guide the audience towards accepting the meaning *preferred* by the maker of the text. It is possible to anchor meanings to images in various ways, depending on the medium. Any anchor which is attached to a text fulfils its function and purpose only for that single

Animal friends

occasion. We may see the same image again in a different context where it may have been anchored to a different meaning. The opposite page shows an example of the same image anchored to a meaning by the use of a caption.

You will often see anchoring of images in news and documentary or in magazines. It is a strategy which is carried out to best effect when it is used with advertising images where the written copy, even if it is only a short slogan, leads audiences towards transferring their feelings about the image into the product.

Images can also be anchored by sound including voice-over, dialogue, sound effects or music. Moving images and other sequences of images are anchored by the context set by the whole sequence. As an audience watches a sequence, the number of potential meanings is decreased as new information is added throughout the sequence. One image appearing in isolation remains open to a range of interpretations, whereas a sequence of images limits potential readings by focusing the audience on a more limited interpretation. Thus, the anchoring of images not only guides audiences *towards* particular readings, it also guides them *away* from other possible meanings.

Two levels of meaning

It could be said, therefore, that all images offer audiences at least two levels of meaning:

1 What the image actually shows the audience, i.e. what is denoted.

2 What the image causes the audience to think about when the image is seen, i.e. what is connoted.

The audience's capacity to move between the two levels and how they make sense of what they see is guided by how the image is constructed. For example, on a denotative level we may see a man with a gun, but on a connotative level information gained from his body language, clothing, level of lighting could cause us to think of him as either a criminal, a suicide, a soldier, a policeman or a salesman.

Denotation and **connotation** offer the audience access to non-verbal structures of meaning. Once we see an image, we are immediately working out its meaning for ourselves using the information offered to us on both levels.

When we see a sequence of moving images, we need to process all this information quickly. As shots change, new characters enter or leave, settings change and sounds are added, the range of possible connotations which the audience may draw changes from scene to scene.

Denotation is within the control of the producer of the text. Connotation often depends on two things:

> 1 The audience's existing knowledge of how things work within a particular media form, or particular type of story.
>
> 2 Knowledge held by individual members of the audience which allows them to draw on their own life experience and bring it to bear on their understanding of what is denoted.

ACTIVITY 4.1   Analysing an image

The image below is a section of a larger picture. The original image has been cropped, that is cut down, so that part of it can be used.

1 Describe what you can see in as much detail as possible. Remember to think about the background, expression on the man's face and other details.
2 Why do you think this photograph was taken?
3 What do you expect to see when the rest of the photograph is revealed?

Here is another section of the same photograph.

4 Describe what you can see in as much detail as possible, not forgetting the background.

5 What are the possible connections between the first and second parts of the photograph?

6 Where do you think these two parts of the photograph might fit together as parts of the larger image?

7 Has the new information offered in the second section caused you to change what you expect to see in the whole photograph?

8 What do you expect to see in the whole frame?

This is the whole photograph from which the first two sections have been taken.

9 Describe the whole image.
10 Is it what you expected to see?
11 Have you had to revise your original understanding of the section which you saw first?
12 Who do you now think took the photograph? For what purpose?
13 What different captions could be used to anchor meanings to this image?

Codes

Barthes believed that certain signs occur so often that they pass out of the state of being only signs and become **codes** with several complex layers of meaning attached to them. Codes develop when they reach a point where there is a common implicit agreement among members of a society about what certain codes mean or stand for. A simple example is the signifier 'grey suit' which carries within it a reference to the code of 'men in grey suits', which may cause us to think about power, bureaucracy, organisation. When you read the section in this book about stereotyping, you may find it easier to understand if you refer back to this section on signs and codes.

Moving images

The same methods of encoding information are present in moving images. You should read the chapters in this book on narrative and representation before you begin to look at how the construction of moving-image material can be analysed, or deconstructed. This is because when you analyse moving images you will also need to consider how images operate in relation to the following:

- sequence
- place within the narrative
- type of narrative/genre
- media form
- purpose of the text
- lighting
- camera positioning and movement
- sound including dialogue, music and sound effects
- language
- repetition of certain signs and symbols throughout the text
- representation of people, places and objects.

5 | **NARRATIVE**

An understanding of **narrative** is essential for students of the media because *every* text has a narrative. The *Oxford English Dictionary* defines narrative as 'tale, story, recital of facts'.

Storytelling surrounds us; everybody tells stories and has done since childhood. We are incapable of *not* telling stories, even when there is nobody to listen. We order our thoughts and conversations by using our ability to impose coherence, logical sequences, on a world where we are bombarded at random by fragments of information. Our ever-present need for understanding, knowledge and control drives us to use our knowledge of narrative to help us to make sense of our experiences and of the world. We create stories from seemingly unconnected events; invent histories for objects and devise backgrounds for people we meet. We explain, clarify, organise or interpret events for ourselves and for other people. This text is itself an attempt to do that.

Constructing a narrative

Narratives offered to audiences in media forms do much of the hard work of connecting and organising events and thoughts for us. The audience participates in media narratives by making interpretations, based on previous knowledge and experience as well as on information given in the text. Each text becomes part of both the previous and the following one through its relationship with the audience. Texts become interconnected. We may interpret some texts only or mostly through knowledge that we have gained through the media. For example, nobody alive now has personal experience of what life was like in the seventeenth century. Yet we have some *idea* of what it was like, from contemporary texts, which historians call sources, and from texts created later which attempt to offer us ways to understand the contemporary material. In either case, whether we are consulting contemporary or later material as audience or as student, we are dealing with a constructed narrative. This narrative is open to interpretation, because some aspects have been selected to remain in the narrative, while others have been excluded or deselected as being redundant to the version of the story being told.

As members of an audience or readers of history books we do not expect to have to work as hard to understand the narrative outline of our chosen text as we expect to work at understanding our own first-hand experiences. We expect to be able to engage with media narratives quickly, and to find them entertaining, interesting, amusing, informative or controversial. For example, when reading a newspaper article or watching a television documentary we expect to find logical links between one event and another, tied to images that reinforce what we read or hear. If we are watching a television comedy or cinema film we expect the narrative to move through time and space with characters whose motivation is clear to us. Successful stories rely on actions and events which cause some change to take place in the lives of the people in the story. If nothing happens, there is no story to be told.

Unlike ourselves in our daily lives, makers of media texts are able to select and control most elements which make up the final version of their narrative. When making a fictional narrative they can create characters, places and events, predict the future of these elements and *make it happen*. Audiences are presented with a finished product which consists only of what the makers have decided to include.

This element of construction is present both in texts which tell fictional stories, and in texts which are presented as news and documentary, because these are produced after the actual events have taken place. Even 'live' broadcasts are planned, managed and edited as the broadcast progresses, in an attempt to ensure that the audience receives a coherent narrative. Although the people, places and events are not 'made up' in news and documentary, it is important to be aware that the reports we see, hear and read are constructed narratives.

Conventions

To study narrative, rather than simply to understand what narrative is, it is necessary to look at how different conventions and codes have developed in various media forms, and how we as members of an audience are able to decode and understand them. In this sense, 'convention' is used to describe the agreed, accepted or standard practice used when conveying particular types of information to an audience. For example, different types, or **genres**, of film use different conventions to create characters and atmospheres appropriate to the stories they tell.

Conventions have become an important part of the structure of all media texts, because they allow the audience to understand quickly and clearly the information offered to them. By looking behind the surface of the text at the framework of events portrayed and the production techniques used to tell the story, media students are able to study the conventions of narrative construction, and in particular to study:

- how narratives construct time, people, places and events
- how audiences' interest is engaged
- why narratives have an effect on audiences
- how meanings are constructed by audiences
- how the organising principles of narrative can be used to create different types of narrative within and across media forms.

Codes

Roland Barthes worked on how information is encoded into texts. His interest was in how audiences are able to decode and understand texts. He devised a way of analysing the information in texts by organising the elements into a series of 'codes'. Two of these are related to narrative development:

- the *action code*, also known as the *proiaretic code*, is used to signal major events or significant moments in story development.
- the *enigma code* (or *hermeneutic code*) is used to establish how much the audience knows about the plot and story at any given moment, that is, to study how media producers create an involvement in the story based on the audience's lack of knowledge about what might happen next.

Barthes also defined three other methods of encoding information. His semic, referential and symbolic codes can be applied to the form and style of the text and this requires detailed reference to what we see within the frame of the text. It was Barthes' belief that audiences make sense of texts within the framework of their own experiences and knowledge. Thus it is possible for images to act as symbols (that is, to stand for another thing) or cultural references (that is, to refer to something which can remind an audience of other experiences). Or they can simply describe or reproduce something.

Structure

This method of approaching media texts assumes that there is an underlying structure which can be uncovered and that elements of this structure are common to all narratives.

The work of Tzvetan Todorov is of interest here, as it offers one way of considering how narratives are structured. Todorov studied the action of narrative, that is how stories develop and what motivates this development. He proposed that at the beginning of every story there is a state of balance or equilibrium; this state is somehow disrupted by an event, causing loss of balance or disequilibrium; characters realise and recognise that things are no longer as they should be; characters try to put things right. When everybody's efforts are finished a new, usually slightly different, equilibrium has been established. Media students should be concerned with the process of narrative progression and with studying what has changed, been added or lost by the change in equilibrium.

Another method of analysing narrative structure was devised by Vladimir Propp whose work in the 1920s concentrated on the role and functions of the characters within narratives. Propp chose to work with fairy tales, yet much of his work is relevant to contemporary media texts. Propp identified 31 types of action which can be carried out by characters. He defined these actions as 'functions'. Propp also identified a group of characters which he thought were common to all narratives who each perform certain of these functions within a given narrative. Propp's work serves to draw the media student's attention to the central role of character in developing narrative.

Character types and their functions:

- *Hero* – is the seeker.
- *Villain* – opposes the hero.
- *Donor* – provides an object to help the hero.
- *Dispatcher* – provides information which causes the hero to start the journey.

- *False hero* – may be mistaken for the hero as the person to solve the problems.
- *Helper* – helps the hero.
- *Princess* – target for the villain and reward for the prince.
- *Father* – rewards the hero.

Actions or events and their functions:

- The initial situation in a community/family/kingdom.
- A warning is given.
- The warning is ignored.
- A villain appears.
- Things start to go wrong.
- Somebody in the community/family/kingdom is harmed by the villain.
- Somebody in the community/family/kingdom wants or needs something.
- The hero sets out to provide it.
- The hero leaves.
- He is tested, does well and receives an object or person to help him.

- The action moves to a new place.
- There is a struggle between hero and villain.
- The hero is marked.
- The villain is beaten.
- The problem is resolved.

- The hero returns to the community/family/kingdom.
- The hero is pursued.
- He escapes or is rescued.
- A false hero arrives.
- A test is set for the hero and he passes.

- The true hero is recognised.
- The false hero is discredited and punished.
- The hero is rewarded.

ACTIVITY 5.1

Consider the list of characters and functions given above then apply them as far as you can first to a fairy tale, then to any feature film or single drama of your own choice. You may not find an exact fit if you apply Propp's theories to contemporary texts, but they should provide you with a useful starting point when thinking about narrative structures.

Another important theory when thinking about narrative structures comes from the work of Claude Levi-Strauss. He suggested that narratives are provided with motivation to move from one point to the next by the repeated establishing of actual or potential conflict. He thought that film narratives contain elements which can be paired according to how they oppose each other. For example, during the opening shots of *Jurassic Park* we can see the following 'pairs':

- movement/stillness
- light/dark
- clear shots of men/obscured shots of something unidentified
- human beings/machines
- control/panic.

These opposing pairs provide motivation for the story to develop, as the elements act upon each other and conflict is the result. The way in which characters try to resolve these conflicts creates the narrative. Levi-Strauss called these 'pairs' binary oppositions.

ACTIVITY 5.2

Watch the beginning of any feature film and note down any pairs of oppositions which occur. Remember to consider the soundtrack as well as what you can see.

Deconstruction

To reveal the structure of a given text, it is possible to reduce it to its constituent parts for analysis, or to **deconstruct** the text. That is, to consider separately the individual parts which were assembled during the production of the text. To deconstruct a text is to attempt to undo, or see behind the work of media producers. Most producers of mainstream media texts purposely disguise their production techniques. After all, the point of creating a film narrative is to offer audiences a piece of work where the 'joins' are invisible and where the methods of making the text do not interfere with the audience's reception and enjoyment of the narrative.

Plot and story

There is a difference between the story and the **plot** of a narrative. This is one of the easiest aspects of narrative structure to uncover. Think of any feature film you know well – it probably does not relate the whole story to the audience in chronological order, but leaves the audience without certain pieces of information. At some points in the narrative some characters know things which other characters do not know. Both audience and characters become involved in making sense of the events and information in the order in which they are given. This method of organising events is called plotting.

ACTIVITY 5.3

1 For a film which you know well, note down the following:
   a) the order in which events occur;
   b) the order in which each of the main characters finds out about these events.
2 Compare this list to the chronological order of events, as if you were telling someone else what happened in the film. The difference between the two will enable you to see clearly how the technique of plotting works.

The device of plotting encourages the audience to remain interested in the story as it unfolds because, for example, we want to know what will happen when the children find out that Mrs. Doubtfire is really their father, or whether the Mariner will discover the meaning of the child's tattoo in *Waterworld*.

Narration

The role of *who* is telling the story, that is, from whose viewpoint the audience is told the tale, is crucial to the study of narrative. It is the job of the narrator to tell the story to the audience, or narrattee. Most narratives may be told in the third or the first person, either by a character who did not take part in the events, or by a character who participated in some way in the onscreen events (e.g. Philip Marlow in *The Big Sleep*). Some narratives are told from more than one point of view and may shift between the third and first-person narrator. Where no character is assigned the role of narrator, the audience usually assumes a third person to be telling the story.

The narrator has several functions:

- to tell the events which make up the story
- to mediate the events for the audience
- to evaluate those events for the audience.

We allow the narrator to structure our understanding and accept that the narrator is genuine and 'acting in good faith'. Occasions where the narrator does not do this are rare. We can be influenced in our response to the narrative by our attitude to the narrator. The narrator's dialect, accent, race, gender, or tone of voice may all be used by the film-maker to position the audience in a particular relationship with the characters and events seen.

Time

Media narratives do not take place in real time, but in 'narrative time', sometimes called 'screen time'. This is a self-evident truth which may seem hardly worth mentioning, yet audiences can remain unaware of how time can be manipulated and managed in film and television, and how this influences the way we respond to and make sense of what we see. The average length of a feature film is 90 minutes, and we may see events from years of the characters' lives, yet we do not question this. Instead, we simply accept the conventions which convey to us that time is passing, decode them and make sense of what we see.

For example, in *Citizen Kane*, we accept that years have passed when we see characters age from one shot to another. Similarly, we accept that the next time we see Indiana Jones he will be in the Middle East because we have just seen a shot of an aeroplane superimposed on a map of the world where a red line moves from west to east (from left to right across the screen). We believe that Glen Miller has completed a tour of the United States because we have seen a series of front pages from local newspapers which have told us how successful the concerts have been. We accept that characters leave one location and appear in another with no apparent journey time between. This compression of time, or ellipsis, is offered to audiences through conventions which the audience decodes without question. The effect is to keep the narrative moving and to keep us interested as we move through time with the narrative.

Time can also be manipulated in other ways to facilitate the development of the plot. For example, flashbacks, dream sequences, repetition or reconstruction of events from the viewpoints of different characters (or even from the same viewpoint as in *Groundhog Day*), real-time interludes, flashforwards and the pre-figuring of events which have not yet happened on the screen in the mind of a character are all devices which enable directors to move audiences through time.

Thus, in *Back to the Future* we can accept Marty McFly moving back through time and meeting his parents when they were teenagers, and in *Citizen Kane* we can understand Kane's continuing motivation because it is explained to the audience through flashbacks. The ordering of time is a central element of the construction of film and television narrative which is rarely the subject of explicit discussion.

ACTIVITY 5.4

Watch an episode of any television soap opera.
How is time manipulated within this episode?

Onscreen space

All media narratives are located somewhere. They may take place in real locations (for example, a news item filmed outside the White House, Washington D.C.) or in fictional locations, for example a reconstruction of a saloon in 1880s Texas. Whether fiction, news or documentary is being made the only options available to producers are to use a real location or to build a set. New technology has recently made it possible for virtual sets to be constructed using computers and holograms. In the UK, the BBC's set for the *Nine o'Clock News* is an example of this.

The choice of spaces is often dictated by the type or genre of story being told, or may be influenced by other factors such as availability, cost or distance. Sometimes the availability of particular locations can influence the product. For example, the style of film known as '*film noir*' was created when producers realised that sets built for films being shot during the day were unused at night. By using low lighting and different camera work, film-makers could use the same sets at night to shoot a second film – audiences rarely recognised this double use of sets.

Mise-en-scène

When thinking about cinematic spaces, it is important to remember that film and television narratives are constructed. Whether a production uses locations or sets, it is reasonable to assume that everything we see within the frame has been included on purpose, however fleetingly the camera may rest on it. The building and dressing of a set or location is a painstaking and expensive undertaking. Since media institutions do not wish to waste either time or money, they do not pay people to design sets and costumes or to seek out objects which do not actively contribute to the development of the narrative. What media producers seek is to create sets or transform locations into places where the characters seem at home, which add to rather than subtract from the credibility of the narrative. The places must also seem to be real to audiences, that is, a room in a film should look and feel like a real place to the spectator, even if it is really only a three-sided box built from hardboard.

When the physical construction of a set is too obvious the audience is unable to enter the world created in the text, as it is hard to accept the characters and how they behave if the set is not credible. Audiences expect the places they see to bear a resemblance to real life, that is, audiences demand a high degree of verisimilitude to be created for them. This is achieved by the assembly of objects within spaces, lighting, dress and costume, make-up and the behaviour of characters. As members of an audience we usually notice this putting together of narrative spaces only if something seems to be 'wrong', for example a zip fastener in a costume drama set in the sixteenth century or an aeroplane in a shot of an American Civil War battle scene. Instances like these cause the audience temporarily to set themselves outside the text, and disrupt their willingness and ability to enter into the world created by the text.

The process of preparing and controlling what is seen within the frame is part of what is known as the **mise-en-scène** of a production. Literally it is the putting into place of everything which is needed to stage an event. The concept of mise-en-scène originated in the theatre, but it is a useful way of thinking about the elements which are shown within the frame of film and television texts.

Offscreen space

Media producers also make use of what is known as 'offscreen' space; that is, the spaces that are implied to be around the frame which we see. The six areas of offscreen space are:

- above the frame
- below the frame
- to the left of the frame
- to the right of the frame
- behind the frame
- behind the camera.

It is possible for directors to make use of these implied spaces by having characters refer to them. Characters might, for example:

- look out of the frame towards another character who is about to enter the frame;
- leave the frame through a door at the back of the set which actually leads nowhere;
- hear a voice from offscreen which reminds the audience of the spaces around the frame.

Of all these spaces, the one behind the camera is the most difficult to convey, and is therefore the least used of these implied spaces. An example of this can be seen in Jean Renoir's *La Regle du Jeu* (*The Rules of the Game*), 1939.

Light

The skill of lighting the space within the frame is a major part of the construction of moving-image narrative. The lighting gives the audience information about the time of day or night, the season, the weather, and whether the characters are inside or outside. Lighting can also give the audience clues to character which offer insights into people, places and things within the frame.

Choice of film stock also affects the final look of the film, as 'faster' film is more sensitive to light than 'slow' film. Lighting is sometimes used to draw the audience's attention towards a particular part of the frame at different times; our eyes are more readily attracted to well-lit areas than to shadowy areas. This is achieved by balancing areas of high and low light, light and shadow, clarity and obscurity. The angle at which light enters the frame, and its intensity creates atmosphere, which in turn guides audience reactions to particular places, people or objects. To take an extreme example a character whose face is lit from below is often, at that point in the text, seen as shadowy and sinister, whereas characters who are lit from the side are more natural looking and may be thought of as less threatening.

Shots

Most of the decisions about what a moving image text will look like when it is finished are made at the planning stages of any production. The actual telling of the story finally depends on how the film is shot and later edited. It is the action of the film, what is happening in the foreground, which mostly concerns the audience. However well dressed the set is, or complicated the arrangement of narrative time, we are interested in stories because they are about people. We want to see what happens to them and how they feel about it. For audiences to be able to experience this involvement, directors choose from a fairly limited range of techniques which can convey what they want us to know. These have developed into the standard visual conventions of constructing a narrative.

A shot can be defined as what is filmed, recorded or 'taken' between the time the camera is turned on and turned off again. These shots, or takes, are reviewed at the end of a session of filming and whole or part sequences are selected to be included in the final version of the text. Some takes may be shortened or edited out altogether at the post-production stage of assembling the final version. Several shots are assembled to create a scene; many scenes are used to create the entire narrative.

Most scenes are shot according to a notional 'axis of action' which assumes that characters in the same scene are connected by an imaginary line. The camera is always kept on the same side of this line to ensure a consistency of direction when, for example, two characters are in conversation. Thus in all the shots of a particular scene, each character will have a constant direction to face: character A will look from left to right throughout a scene, and character B will look from right to left. This convention is sometimes called the 180-degree rule, that is to say that the camera is not moved round a character through more than 180 degrees of an imaginary circle of which the character is the fixed centre.

Within a given scene a number of different types of shots can be used. The most common pairing of shots is the sequence known as the 'shot reverse-shot', for example the audience sees a shot of a woman speaking, followed by a shot of the person to whom she is speaking. Thus, the second shot reverses the viewpoint seen in the first shot. This mini- sequence of paired shots is often repeated many times within a scene. It is used to establish a relationship between characters, and is often used with another technique known as 'eyeline matching'. This technique creates the illusion that when characters shown in one shot look out of the frame they are looking directly at who or what we see in the next shot. By matching the height and direction of the character's gaze to the subject of the following shot, continuity is created for the spectator through shooting and editing techniques.

The convention of matching action between shots is also one which audiences understand easily. For example, a character may start an action in one shot and continue it in the next, causing the audience to assume continuity of time and space between the two shots.

The frequency with which certain types of shots are used is also important. Usually, information is given to the audience only once, as that is enough to progress the narrative. However, when the director thinks that a point needs emphasising, information may be repeated. This technique is related to the construction of screen-time, for repetition often relies on the use of flashbacks, or the recounting of an event which the audience has already seen, from the viewpoint of a second character.

Another convention is the use of establishing shots, which we mostly see at the start of a narrative, or at the beginning of a new segment within it. Such shots set the scene in which the action is to take place, and make the audience aware of places and how characters relate to them. After the action, for example following a conversation, we usually see a re-establishing shot, which redefines the place for the audience. The narrative may then move to a different place, which, of course, requires its own establishing shot.

The camera

The positioning of the camera is the most important thing to be aware of when deconstructing a film or television narrative. The camera frames everything we see, and we see only those things which can be contained within the viewfinder. We see them from the point of view, height and distance chosen by the director. Compare this to the experience of going to the theatre. Although a play may be staged with the intention of directing the audience's attention towards the protagonists at important dramatic moments, members of the audience are free to look elsewhere. The director of a film or television programme can ensure that an audience sees exactly what he or she wants them to see by using, for example, an extreme close-up which fills the screen. Although we know that we, the audience, are behind the camera, we rarely discuss this. What we do discuss is what we see, because we enter into an unspoken agreement with the text to treat it as if it is reality; we agree to allow the means of production to remain invisible.

Choices about positioning the camera are central to audience response because our perception of anything and anyone within the frame changes as the camera is positioned and re-positioned. We may be moved closer to or further away from a character or object; we may suddenly be shown a place or object from an unexpected or different angle. For example, a car chase shot from above may be exciting to watch, but shot from inside the car being pursued it may make us feel threatened and afraid. Similarly, a scene shot from behind a person holding a gun, in which we are positioned to witness events from the assassin's point of view is less threatening to the audience than the same event shot from the point of view of the intended victim.

We understand that a series of shots of the same place, or a continuous shot which takes us ever closer, to single out one building from among many, conveys the importance of that place to the narrative. For example, a wide shot of a town which is cut to a shot of one street, then to one house, then to a front door makes the audience aware that this door and what lies behind it will be central to the events which are to follow. It also pulls us in to the story on a visual level.

Similarly, the choice of height and angle (either straight on, high or low) of shooting can affect how we make sense of parts of the narrative. A car chase shot from above positions the audience outside the tensions experienced by the characters involved in the chase, as the audience become observers rather than participants in the urgency of the chase. A scene which shows a body falling to the ground will affect the audience differently if it is shot from a low angle, below the body as it hurtles towards the ground and the audience, than if it is shot from a high angle, which would show the body plummeting away from the audience.

Camera movement

The camera is not always still. Apart from the common technique of zooming towards or away from the subject, we often see vertical or horizontal movement. By panning the camera from side to side, or tilting the camera up and down, different effects can be achieved. In these shots the camera lens alone, not the whole camera, is moved around at a fixed point.

The whole camera can also be moved along the ground while filming. When it is moved in this way, we see a tracking shot, so named because tram-lines or tracks are built especially to accommodate the planned movement of the camera. When the camera is moved up or down above ground level, it is usually fixed to a crane, hence this is called a crane shot. In both tracking and crane shots the camera is held steady.

Sometimes the camera is not held steady, but is hand-held, so that filming reflects the movements of the camera operator. This technique usually gives the audience a more subjective view of proceedings than steady camera work. All such movements of the camera are known collectively as mobile framing.

The choices made by directors about the height, angle and distance from the subject when framing a shot, positions the audience in certain places throughout the narrative. We understand that we move from position to position because we have become familiar with these shooting conventions. If we were not familiar with them it would be almost impossible for us to make sense of what we see.

Editing

Few film or television texts are shot in the order in which they will appear on screen. The final version is constructed according to the original planning of the production. This is done according to outline 'treatments' of the story, storyboarding for sound, vision and action and a final 'shooting script' which contains detailed directions about how every aspect of the production is to be created. Editing is the physical process of joining the film containing the surviving shots and their soundtrack.

The purpose of editing is to assemble individual shots into a **sequence** which audiences can read as a coherent narrative. This usually means that shots are arranged so that they progress the narrative in an order suggested by cause-and-effect logic and that there is some motivation for characters to behave in the way they do. The technique of editing to these ends is usually called *continuity editing* because it creates a continuous narrative. The techniques of production are kept invisible, thus enabling the audience to be drawn into the world of the narrative. Successful continuity editing hides the textual spaces between place and time. As spectators we are able to accept consecutive shots which may move across time and place or cut between different characters. The logic created within the narrative makes us willing to make sense of the jumps and spaces because we know that they are necessary to the progress of the story, rather than disrupting it.

The duration, or time, for which a shot is onscreen in screen time, and therefore the speed at which a sequence of shots passes before the audience are an important part of the editing at post-production. This process dictates the pace at which the story unfolds and is used to create different rhythms for different parts of the narrative. A different pace causes a change in the audience's understanding of and response to a sequence of shots. For example, a series of very short takes edited together may create a feeling of tension or excitement, whereas a series of long takes is more likely to induce calm or thoughtfulness.

Page two

SHOT	CUE	CAM. & ANGLE	SET	ACTION
		(Tilt up to centre)		and tilt up to centre. Those, then, were some of the basic camera moves. One can also achieve the effect of movements through the use of a Zoom lens.
6	CUT	CAM 3	CAPTION SLIDE of lens turret	In the past, several lenses of varying focal length were mounted on a turret so that the subjects appeared to vary in distance from the camera.
7	CUT	CAM 1 M C/U	PRESENTER	The disadvantage of this lens system was that the lenses could not be changed on shot. Today, the use of a zoom means that the focal length of the lens may be changed continuously from telephoto to wide angle. Provided that the distance between the camera and the subject is not changed, re-focussing is unnecessary and the zoom may take place on shot.
8	CUT	CAM 2 L/S	PRESENTER	The zoom lens allows the cameraman to change the camera angle without necessarily moving the camera. This shot is termed a long shot.
9	SUPER	CAM 2 L/S CAM 3	PRESENTER CAPTION SLIDE Long shot	See how it includes all the surroundings, leaving the subject relatively small in the frame.
10	CUT	CAM 1 M/S	PRESENTER	A medium shot is one in which the subject is shown from waist level up.
11	SUPER	CAM 1 M/S CAM 3	PRESENTER CAPTION (Slide) Medium shot.	It is sometimes referred to as a mid-shot.
12	CUT	CAM 2 C/U	PRESENTER	Finally, the subject can be shown in close-up with the head and the top of the shoulders filling the screen.

Example page from a shooting script

6 REPRESENTATION AND REALITY

It is important to make an explicit distinction between reality and media **representations** and to remember that the media operate in the spaces between the viewing, listening or reading audience and the world outside. The media are systems through which we experience the world beyond the space we occupy. We could also express this idea by saying that the media construct a relationship between the audience and the real world; they mediate between us and reality and create a version of reality for our consumption.

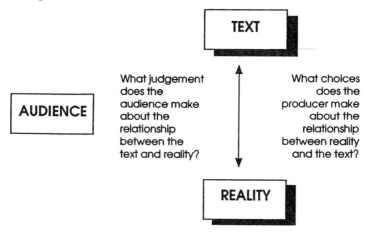

Common sense

Our common-sense, daily use of language allows us to say 'I saw lions on the TV'. This is a good enough description of media experience for daily life, but it is too vague a statement to satisfy the media studies student. Such a general statement ignores the following issues which are concerned with the media and its representations:

- how we understand representations;
- how we talk about them;
- how the programme-maker has chosen to represent the lions to the audience;
- that when we 'see lions on TV' we see pictures of real lions, not real lions themselves.

Some lions

It is possible to clarify this standpoint by considering the case of documentary. In making a documentary about lions, the programme-makers have done two things simultaneously. They have brought lions to our living room, thereby extending our experience of the real world, and they have selected for us what they think it is important for us know about lions, thereby restricting our experience of the real world. What is selected for inclusion in the documentary depends on the viewpoint being taken, and the points that the producers wish to convey to the audience. It would be more accurate to say 'I saw some representations of lions on the TV'.

You may see other representations of lions at other times. Different programme-makers may choose to represent lions to audiences in different ways. Some examples of the ways in which lions may be represented to audiences are as savage beasts, as a threatened species, or as larger versions of the domestic cat. It is unlikely that any of these representations can give audiences all the knowledge which is available about lions, prepare audiences adequately to meet a lion, or even bring audiences close to the programme-makers' own experience of having filmed or met lions. All they are able to do is to offer us some information about lions and attempt to use the medium to bring audiences close to the film-makers' own experiences and perceptions.

It is vital to keep in mind this relationship between reality and the representations of reality which the mass media offer us. What we, the consumers of media texts, actually see are representations of reality; images which stand in the place of the real things and people in the world, and which we as the audience might take for reality itself. Representations can show us a partial reality or aspects of the real thing which have been selected for the audience by producers.

Truth or fiction?

The debate about whether media representations offer audiences truth or fiction may seem to be an obvious starting point. Everybody knows that pictures are not real, that they are only images of real things. Many people say that they don't believe what they see on the television or read in the newspapers, while treasuring family photographs or videos of family events, which they feel do record 'truth'. Where belief is concerned we draw a distinction between our personal media productions and texts produced by others which are intended for mass circulation. This is perhaps because we do know the answers to such questions as 'Who made this and why did they make it?' when we are looking at family photographs. The answers are harder to come by when we do not know the producer of a text.

As individuals and as a society we also draw a distinction between what we call 'fiction' and what we think of as 'non-fiction'. As audiences, we hold two points of view at once: that media texts are both true and not true. We each believe that we are in a position to decide what to categorise as real or true and what to categorise as made-up. We are proud that we can make up our own minds about fiction, non-fiction and how realistic mass-media products are, and most of us spend a great deal of time doing so.

However, this approach to media representations can cause a problem for the media studies student, because it is easy to become side-tracked into searching for an elusive truth which may never be found, let alone proven.

A different approach

The media studies student can begin to solve this problem about truth and fiction by taking a different approach to the issue. This can be achieved by starting to think about representations within texts regardless of how we might categorise the text itself in terms of fiction or non-fiction. If we take as a starting point the fact that all texts are constructed, the questions we ask about texts can then be moved away from debates about truth or fiction. Instead, we can consider producers' choices and audiences' interpretations or decoding of the meanings of the chosen representations.

For example, the media studies student would not ask if a representation were 'true' but would ask some or all of the following questions:

- Who made this representation?
- Who or what is represented?
- How are the people or objects represented?
- Why was this image, or series of images, chosen rather than another representation?
- Do I have an existing context which I can use to understand the representation?

The justification for this approach is based on an understanding of the nature of how texts are constructed (see Chapter 5). By looking at who and what is represented and how they are represented, we can analyse how a text has been put together, what implied shared knowledge it relies upon in order for the audience to understand it and what conclusions we, the audience, might draw about what we have seen.

Looking at representations

ACTIVITY 6.1   Photographs

Look carefully at the images opposite, then answer the questions which follow:

1 Describe the people in these images.
2 Describe the setting.
3 What kind of people are they?
4 How do you feel about them?
5 Would you like to meet them?
6 What reasons can you give for your reactions?
7 Can you say whether these are stills from documentary or fictional material?
8 Does it matter?

The power of representation

You might be wondering what all the fuss is about. Why is it important to think about representations, when it's obvious to everyone that representation is what the media are *about*? We have thought about representations as sources of information in terms of the invented documentary about lions, and have considered how such a programme might extend the audience's frame of reference and knowledge base. This offering of knowledge can be seen as mostly unproblematic in the context of wildlife documentary making.

However, if we were to think about a documentary covering a current-affairs issue or about a news bulletin, the ways in which people, events and ideas are represented to the audience takes on an extra dimension. It is at this point that the audience's frame of reference becomes crucially important. By using their existing knowledge audiences are able to question the mediated reality offered to them. For example, individuals may have additional information from other sources which they can use to amplify, or even challenge the content of a news item.

It is important here to remember that the producers of news and documentary, whether in print or on the screen or radio, select their representations of people, places, events and ideas in terms of the viewpoint to be expressed in the text. This viewpoint is not necessarily isolated from the beliefs or ideology of the individuals responsible for producing the text, or from the institution which employs them. Nor is a text *necessarily* made with the intention of explicitly promoting a set of beliefs. Every text operates within a series of different contexts which are created by writers, editors, producers, interviewees, schedulers and the audience. Every institution has a different standpoint which is reflected to a greater or lesser extent in each of its products. This inclusion of a viewpoint is sometimes the result of a conscious decision to reflect the attitudes and values of an institution, but may be an indirect result of the way staff are selected and recruited, or of the criteria used to agree content. An investigation of why certain representations are chosen can lead us to an understanding of how beliefs, or ideologies can be expressed through the content of texts.

ACTIVITY 6.2 Representing the news

Reproduced on the following six pages are some of the front pages of British national daily newspapers for Tuesday 18 March 1997, the day after a general election was called in the United Kingdom for 1 May. Every newspaper made the election its main story, and each of them except the *Daily Mail* featured at least one image related to the story.

Look carefully at the images on the newspaper front pages, reproduced on the following pages, and use them to focus your thoughts on what you have read in this chapter about representing the news. The questions which follow should help you to structure your response.

1 Which newspapers have only photographs?
2 Which have only cartoons or diagrams?
3 Which have both?
4 Which front page do you find the most interesting?
5 Can you say why you have chosen this one?
6 How is John Major, Prime Minister at the time, represented in the photographs?
7 How is Tony Blair, Leader of the Opposition at the time, represented in the photographs?
8 Which headlines directly refer the reader to the images accompanying the story?
9 Which headlines refer to the images only indirectly?

Realism

Realism is often associated with the issues discussed here in relation to representations. Criticisms are often levelled at texts which are seen to be insufficiently realistic, and other texts are praised because they are judged by audiences to be realistic. This judgement is, of course, subjective in many cases. Realism has little to do with reality and a lot to do with how people, places and events are represented in texts. Realism is actually little

THE TIMES

35p

No. 65,840   TUESDAY MARCH 18 1997

PLAY THE £50,000 GAME
See how your players are performing
PAGES 50, 51

INSIDE:
EIGHT-PAGE ELECTION PULL-OUT
Full guide to the general election
PAGES 11-19

DAY TWO:
The intellectual Hollywood hunks
PLUS
Why sex is so dangerous PAGES 22, 23

Major and Blair hit campaign trail

Early blows for Tories as leaders meet the people

By PHILIP WEBSTER, POLITICAL EDITOR

JOHN MAJOR climbed back onto his soapbox. Tony Blair went vote hunting in the constituency that could put him into Downing Street. The bureau for a May 1 general election had been pressed.

The leaders hit the campaign trail within hours of the Prime Minister's announcement that Parliament would rise on Friday, and Mr Major clearly relished the prospect of a "fun campaign" which he insisted was winnable.

But he suffered a double jolt when The Sun announced that it would be backing Mr Blair and a Gallup poll for The Daily Telegraph gave Labour a 26-point lead. No party has ever been so far ahead at the start of an election campaign. The Sun, which claimed in 1992 that its anti-Labour stance returned the Conserva-

John Major got back on his soapbox (below) to address voters at Luton yesterday, where he braved heckling from protesters. The Prime Minister promised a "fun campaign"

for the next seven weeks he would be "there in the middle of the crowd".

Labour was straddling a "chasm of credibility", he said, and he urged his party to help him to tip it into the "yawning abyss below". Later, in a special statement, he added: "Either you stick with a party you know about and policies that have worked, or you take a leap into the dark, with a party that you don't know and which doesn't want you to know what its policies are."

Mr Blair was visiting a school in south London when the election announcement came. He then travelled west to meet voters in Gloucester — where a Labour victory would point to an overall majority in the Commons.

"We are on the verge of a new millennium. There is so much this country can do. So much talent, resource and energy among its people," he said. "I want a new government to come in with different values and priorities to lead a national renewal which will be at the heart of everything we want to achieve."

Mr Blair matched Mr Major's assertion that it would be a meet-the-people campaign and rejected "the presidential style of glitz and glamour" that has been predicted.

But later, in an unguarded moment, he was caught on camera saying: "How the great campaign has begun, we can carry on with this for another six weeks which will drive us all absolutely crazy."

He was speaking after an interview with BBC2's News-night in which he denied that his party switches in the 1980s meant that he did not have the same enthusiasm to be Prime

Continued on page 2, col 7

INSIDE

tives to power, today publishes a front-page editorial describing Mr Blair as the "breath of fresh air" that Britain needs. The Tories are "tired, divided and rudderless" and no longer deserve support, it says.

At the same time, the Telegraph is publishing the results of an opinion poll taken over the weekend and completed after the election announcement yesterday. It showed that 56.5 per cent of those questioned supported Labour — a two-and-a-half point increase on ten days ago — while only 28.5 per cent backed the Conservatives. The Liberal Democrats were on 9.5 per cent. Forty-seven per cent thought Mr Blair would be the best Prime Minister, against 25 per cent favouring Mr Major.

The Prime Minister did, however, receive an early boost from Baroness Thatcher, who emerged from her London office to say: "I am fighting for Prime Minister Major and I am fighting with every effort I can bring forth."

Mr Major started his campaigning in Luton — where he first used the soapbox that proved to be his secret weapon in 1992. He produced it again yesterday and declared that

Back on his soapbox in Middle England

POLITICAL SKETCH

AFTER tea with the Queen it must have made quite a contrast. In Luton town centre yesterday John Major planted himself into a walkabout which teetered perilously close to mayhem as a band of hard-core Militant-style mobsters teamed up with the usual sporty student-demo brigade — "groom suck" — to offer the Prime Minister and the electorate a nostalgic reminder of the way we were 18 years ago. "How much did Major pay these people?" I heard a BBC reporter asking colleagues.

There was something sweetly amateurish about the whole thing. To the trilling of a mobile phone and the heckles of beer-swilling English youths, an 18th-century kind of electioneering over a 20th-century election, perhaps our best.

As news of Mr Major's swoop on Middle England spread, more than a thousand had gathered. Leaping from his green Jaguar near a shop called Going Places, the Prime Minister was quickly engulfed in an extraordinary scrum-team of Tory ladies, gamely cheering "Hurrah!", thin-faced yobs with shoulder bags.

a penne from the Referendum Party — elderly women with sour lips — and a gathering mass of inquisitive shoppers.

Mr Major does what he always does in moments of tension. He started pasting people. After a few immaculately pats he stormed into a bank, ...

of "Five more years" and another of "Give up, John." A tiny boy strained right up a "see-parking" sign as the Prime Minister struggled through to a terrain by a Burger King.

"You're our Bright!" shouted a pair of greasy anoraks at the sitting MP. Sir Graham Bright, took the microphone and declared "Luton is now a prosperous town." But the loudspeakers were faulty and most of the speech sank beneath the loyal cheers of Tory ladies and a chant of "What do we want? More money for students!" Then the Prime Minister mounted his famous soapbox. There was a shout of "ten more years", another of "boring" and then a sort of hush. Mr Major began to speak. "They won't stop the Conservative Party," he declared.

"You're lying!" shouted a Geordie. Then he revised his heckle. "You've got a nerve — but you're lying." It was in some ways the most eloquent tribute of the afternoon.

Some of Mr Major's speech was audible. He looked at times rattled but always determined. As he made his way

towards the waiting cars the police appeared to lose control and he was almost pinned against the Alliance & Leicester Building Society. "More uniforms!" barked a slightly panicky police voice into a walkie-talkie. "Eighteen more years!" shouted one brave lady.

Behind the Prime Minister, they retrieved the wooden soapbox which, should he win this fight, will be parcelled up

and auctioned in bits as holy relics for centuries to come.

At the bus stop outside the tower hall, three troupe of pensioners awaited their bus. Mr Major came, saw and patted. The crowds came. The police came. And, finally, all departed as the prime ministerial Jaguar sped off up the hill. Previously engulfed, the bus stop came back into view. The pensioners were still there, waiting.

Tourist shot

A British tourist from south London has been shot dead in front of his wife after a dispute with a police patrol while travelling through the Congo accompanied by four other Britons.

Nirex plan vetoed

John Gummer vetoed plans by Nirex for a nuclear waste-disposal facility at Gosforth, Cumbria. The scheme had already been rejected by the county council .... Page 4

The Times on the Internet http://www.the-times.co.uk

British nuns flee clinic as armed priest holds off Albanian mob

By ANTHONY LOYD IN TIRANA and MARK HENDERSON

FIVE nuns from a British order fled an armed mob who raised their clinic in the Albanian town of Korce, a spokeswoman for the order said last night.

There were unconfirmed reports that a Canadian priest held off the crowd with a gun until they were able to escape.

The nuns, from the Nottingham-based Little Company of Mary, are now thought to be travelling to Athens or Corfu after resting in the Greek border town of Kastoria. Sister Elizabeth Harmer, 60, is from Ealing in west London, and Sister Anita MacDonald, 50, is from South Uist in the Hebrides; of the other nuns two are Irish and one is Australian.

The sisters were forced to

flee Korce in a van last Thursday as Albania descended into anarchy. They managed to cross the border on Friday despite roadblocks set up outside Kastoria.

The Canadian priest and two other British women — thought to be nuns — have decided to stay in Korce, a Foreign Office spokesman confirmed yesterday. Sister Geraldine Mackin, a spokeswoman for the Little Company of Mary, said last night that the nuns were shaken by their ordeal but otherwise were in good spirits.

"They are determined to get back in there," she said. "They were nursing the only clinic in town which cares for the sick and the dying, and the town needs them more than ever."

Rail guard attacks fat French controllers

By STEPHEN FARRELL

A GUARD had an unexpected announcement for commuters forced to squeeze on to the 7.06 am service from Ashford, Kent, to London Charing Cross.

As the train had only four carriages instead of the usual eight, passengers should, he told them, feel free to pull the emergency cord to register their disapproval.

He also read out the address of the company which runs the South Eastern service, Connex, which is owned by the French Companie Générale des Eaux. According to experts Andrew Watson, 43, also told passengers: "Connex is owned by a group of fat French peasants whose only interest in life is making money. They have no inten-

tion of providing even a half-decent service."

Yesterday, from his council house in Ashford, Mr Watson said: "I deny emphatically saying anything against the French. What I was saying was a serious matter of safety."

After the incident on February 28, Mr Watson was dismissed for gross misconduct at a disciplinary hearing. The company is understood to have evidence from four Connex employees on board the train and one passenger.

A spokesman for Connex said: "The conductor allegedly made inappropriate comments to passengers. He has been dismissed and his case is subject to appeal. We cannot therefore comment further."

CERRUTI 1881

THE INDEPENDENT

Nº 3,247 ★★★★ TUESDAY 18 MARCH 1997 WEATHER: Cloudy early; fine everywhere later 40p

Election '97

THIS PAPER'S MANIFESTO:
HARD FACTS AND STRAIGHT QUESTIONS,
WITH NO PARTY AGENDA AND
NO STRING-PULLING MOGULS.

The man who thinks he can win

Very well, then: alone. John Major defiant yesterday. Within hours, the 'Sun' had deserted him

Anthony Bevins
Political Editor

John Major yesterday opened the 1 May election campaign with an appeal to voters to accept that if it was time for a change, "we are the change". That plea was later reinforced by a warning that the election was no game.

But Tony Blair said: "The Tories keep saying to people that this is the best that Britain can be. What I say to people is that Britain can be better than this."

The Labour leader's appeal was last night backed by the latest in a long line of heavyweight endorsements, with a front-page *Sun* headline saying: "The Sun backs Blair. Give change a chance."

For the Liberal Democrats, Paddy Ashdown welcomed the chance for voters to say what they thought of the Government's "broken promises, incompetence and divisions".

The start of the six-week election campaign was at long last triggered by the Prime Minister with an impromptu Cabinet, a visit to the Palace, and a return to Downing Street, where he announced the election timetable.

Parliament will sit for the rest of this week, clearing an agreed programme of residual legislation before rising on Friday. It will not meet again before being formally dissolved, by proclamation, on 8 April.

Before going out on to the hustings, taking his soap-box from the last election on a visit to Luton – a town with two marginal Tory seats, where he received a rowdy reception from demonstrating students – Mr Major said the Government had, since 1979, given the country "a revolution in choice".

He told reporters in Downing Street that in spite of the "bruises and difficulties" he was proud of his party's 18-year record, before turning to address his biggest weak spot – the argument that it is time for a change.

"If people are looking for change," Mr Major said, "we are the change, and we'll carry forward what we've been doing for the last 18 years."

He said: "I believe this election is winnable. Not only do I think it's winnable, but I think that we are going to win this election."

Later, in a written statement, Mr Major added: "A general election is not some far-away spectator sport – or a TV talk-show. It will affect life behind every front door in the land." What was at stake, he warned, were issues "that touch the cold hard realities of 56 million daily lives".

Mr Blair told Sky News that the voters would remember the Tory promises of 1992, when Mr Major promised tax cuts, and then raised taxes; his promise not to extend VAT to fuel, before doing so; and his promise to bring crime under control, with violent crime still rising.

Labour would make a difference on schools, the health service, crime and jobs. "We aren't just going to have the rewards going to an élite few at the top," he said.

But Mr Blair will be given a morale boost by the support of the *Sun*, which claimed after the last election: "It was the *Sun* wot won it" for Mr Major.

Undoubtedly acting under the direct orders of Rupert Murdoch, his hands-on proprietor, the *Sun*'s editor, Stuart Higgins, told Channel 4 News last night that Mr Blair was "a dynamic, exciting, energetic new leader for this country", while the Tories were "tired out and incapable of governing ... paralysed by their divisions, and it's time for a change". Clearly hurt, Tory sources said last night that the decision was "peculiar", given the paper's background of Euro-scepticism.

In a London speech, the Liberal Democrat leader said: "I am determined that, every day of this campaign, we focus on how to make Britain the world's number-one learning society in the next century."

But the Prime Minister's first public acceptance of Labour's challenge for a televised leadership debate was getting bogged down in the detailed conditions of Mr Major's terms of engagement.

He said at Downing Street: "I very much wish to meet Mr Blair in debate." But he then delivered a series of qualifications that left Labour, the Liberal Democrats and other minority parties significantly dissatisfied.

Explaining why he did not think that he should have to face both Mr Blair and Mr Ashdown, the Conservative leader said: "After the election, either Mr Blair or I will be Prime Minister. I have some sympathy for Mr Ashdown's position.

"I am sure the broadcasters might find some way to involve him, but I think the principal debate will be between the leader of the Labour Party and myself."

A senior Labour source said it was "silly" of broadcasters to respond to that by trying to find ways to accommodate Mr Major's demand for the exclusion of Mr Ashdown.

The source said the public should not be shut out of the debate; a selected audience should be given the opportunity to put questions to the party leaders. As for the Tory preference for one anchorman to chair the debate, Labour said they would prefer a number of prominent media pundits to be given the chance of grilling the leaders, and putting them and their policies under the microscope.

■ The latest Gallup poll for today's *Daily Telegraph* showed an increased Labour lead of 28 percentage points, putting them on 56.5 per cent, compared with 28.5 per cent for the Tories, and 9 per cent for the Liberal Democrats – their lowest Gallup rating since the summer of 1990.

INSIDE

Campaign countdown, pages 5, 6 and 7
Leading article & Letters, page 17
Unsteady markets, page 20
John Redwood, Polly Toynbee, Donald Macintyre
Comment, pages 18, 19

'I'll not vote – it won't change a thing'

Poll position: Pascal Smart
Photograph: Philip Meech

Clare Garner

Persuading Pascal Smart and millions like him to vote on 1 May will be one of the biggest challenges facing John Major and Tony Blair during the election campaign.

The 24-year-old aspiring musician from Croydon, south London, will be following the campaign closely, but only from a position of "amused superiority". He has *no* intention of voting. At the last election more than 9 million voters stayed away from the polls. This time more than 2.5 million under-25s are expected not to vote.

Nothing short of the closure of all nuclear power stations would make Mr Smart change his mind. "I just don't think any of the main parties handle any of the things that are important – especially for young people," he said en route to his evening job as a £120-a-week barman. "I'd put the environment higher on the agenda, [and] the decriminalisation of cannabis and the general treatment of youth. Young people are basically being disenfranchised. We're being paid a slave wage so that the Government can make more money out of us. If Labour get in, which they probably will, they will just be running the same system in a slightly different way, which doesn't really solve anything, because it's the system which is the problem."

Mr Smart voted for "the lesser of two evils" (Labour) at the last election. This time he does not feel he can even do that. "I don't personally trust Tony Blair, mainly because of the fact that he is so insistent that we can trust him. Essentially, all the Labour Party can say is that the Tory party can't lead the country and they can, but they don't say in what way."

There is, he said, a problem with the *status quo*. "Young people are under the impression that ... nothing will ever change. I myself think the only way anything will change is revolution. The existing trend towards large environmental problems will probably cause that."

He has no respect for any of today's politicians. "They don't have any more foresight than wondering what is going to be the most popular policy and appealing to the lowest common denominator," he said.

Mr Smart would, however, be happy to vote for better policies "if anyone came up with any".

He liked the idea of participating in a pre-election television debate. "Oh yes," he said, his eyes lighting up. "I'd ask them questions about the environment, human rights and about how to take the system down, back to its foundations, and back again in a more successful manner."

But to Mr Smart's mind, there is no point in voting. Labour, he said, is going to win anyway. "I don't think it would ... make any difference – except that Croydon is a marginal constituency."

He is not really fussed about the result. "I'll hopefully be leaving the country and buying a remote island in the South Pacific as soon as possible."

Read
THE INDEPENDENT
online every day on AOL
Call 0800 376 5376
for FREE software – quote "Independent"

QUICKLY

Nuclear-waste chaos
Britain's nuclear-waste disposal plans were thrown into confusion last night after the Environment Secretary, John Gummer, rejected plans for an underground radioactive dump near Sellafield. Page 9

An historic choice for Britain – the case against cynicism

Cynicism is cheap. It's important to remember, through the next sound-bitten, media-manipulated six weeks, that this election offers Britain a serious, potentially historic, choice. The result will imprint itself on our lives for years to come. It will affect our individual wealth and opportunities; how we are governed; how we feel about the country.

Yet many millions of us don't agree and have lost interest, never mind faith, in British democracy. In the final years of a turbulent century, which saw the arrival of the full franchise, and the declared victory of democracy across most of the world, a worrying number of Britons have become bored by the whole business. Some 9.6 million adults didn't bother to vote in 1992. This time, many voters have concluded that the country has already made up its mind and won't bother to inquire further.

Yet if the pollsters are vindicated and Tony Blair's New Labour wins on 1 May, then our political system will alter, probably quite fast and probably for ever. From Scotland to London, from Cardiff to Strasbourg, from town halls to the House of Lords, we will see the biggest programme of change to the governance of Britain since before the First World War. Many of these changes will be preceded by referendums. If Mr Blair relies on the Liberal Democrats in government, they will come faster and more strongly than ever. Some excitable souls think they will mean a radical change in the whole party system, giving us a new politics for the millennium. But whatever view you take, it is hardly unimportant.

What, meanwhile, if John Major confounds received opinion, as he has before and, teetering on his soap-box, wins a fifth Conservative term in the teeth of all expectation? That too would mean a changed political system, suggesting the destruction of the Labour Party and the confirmation of one-party government in Britain. It would keep us out of monetary union and ensure a glacial freeze in our relations with continental Union-builders.

These are, without hyperbole, questions of national destiny. But they are only the start. The Tories promise dramatic changes to the Welfare State and pensions, as well as law and order; their domestic programme requires close and detailed scrutiny. Labour has sketched out ambitious-seeming plans for education, employment, youth crime and much else; but "sketched" and "seeming" are the appropriate words. Those goods need a little more scrutiny before the nation buys them.

So there are great issues to be argued over, even if many other issues have been elbowed off the national agenda. Despite everything, our votes remain precious. They should depend on careful thought, narrowed eyes and clear, hard information. That is what we will be bringing you in *The Independent* during the next few weeks – not, I hope, at tedious or sprawling length, but in proper detail and with a due sense of the election's importance and possible consequences.

Our views, as a pro-reform, liberal and open-minded newspaper, biased in favour of enlightenment, have been hammered out by arguing journalists and heckling readers during 10 years. Other papers will be ordered what to say and do, as their proprietors dither between their political convictions and their thirst to be on the winning side. But this paper has full freedom to speak, and no such pressure. This is a great privilege, particularly at election time. We will use it seriously and with relish.

Andrew Marr

CASH IN A FLASH

ABBEYLOAN. THE FAST AFFORDABLE PERSONAL LOAN.

Speed is of the essence, especially if you've already seen something you really want to buy. Abbey National will give you a fast decision on amounts from £500 to £15,000 and our experience will mean you needn't worry about borrowing more than you can afford. All you need to do is pick up the phone and call:

0345 54 55 56
(quoting ref: 7249)

ABBEY NATIONAL DIRECT

CONTENTS

THE BROADSHEET				THE TABLOID			
Business & City	20-24	Home News	2-11	Arts	4,5	Health	8
Comment	17-19	Leading Articles	17	Arts Reviews	11	Listings	12,13
Crossword	28	Letters	17	Crossword	14	Radio & TV	15,16
Foreign News	12-15	Obituaries	16	Culture	2,3	Visual Arts	6,7
		Sport	25-28			Weather	14

12
9 770951 946429

THE ⚔ EXPRESS

FREE INSIDE — THE SPORT — YOUR EXTRA DAILY NEWSPAPER

TUESDAY MARCH 18, 1997
35p

Do women really need HRT?
YourHealth
● PAGE 48

16 BRILLIANT PAGES IN The ⚔ Sport
● PAGE 29

MAJOR'S BACK ON THE BOX

PM brings out a loyal supporter as he throws TV gauntlet to Blair

BY NICHOLAS WOOD
AND SARAH WOMACK

IT has been under wraps for five years. But yesterday John Major got on his soapbox once more to launch his bid for election victory.

After formally announcing May 1 as polling day outside No 10, he made for the streets of marginal Luton — where his trusty prop was first revealed.

Again he faced a rowdy crowd as he reveled in his return to the fray.

Earlier he welcomed for the first time the chance of a live head-to-head debate with Tony Blair on the other box — the TV set.

But appearing on his soapbox — held together with tape — he struggled to make himself heard above the din. He insisted that he would not be deterred by "stunt demonstrators or stunt demonstrations, or the ugly chanting of the-traditional Left".

Tony Blair was also straight on the campaign trail, visiting Gloucester, a seat that Labour must wit to gain outright power.

He called for a new government for the new Millennium and pledged an age of national renewal. But he was taking nothing for granted — dubbing himself the "eternal warrior against complacency".

The Premier's crusade was boosted by a
PAGE 2 COLUMN 2

POLITICAL PLATFORM: Mr Major makes a stand on his venerable election soapbox yesterday during his visit to Luton

INSIDE: OPINION 10 ● WORLD NEWS 14 & 15 ● HICKEY 27 ● CITY 54 ● CROSSWORDS 68 ● TV 69-72 ● WEATHER 70

Daily Mail

TUESDAY, MARCH 18, 1997   35p

NINE PAGES OF GOOD HEALTH START ON PAGE 34

The hi-tech light machine that could cure cellulite

PLUS WIN UP TO £50,000 INSTANT CASH EXTRA TODAY'S AMOUNT PAGE 52

As Major names the day, Murdoch turns against Tories

KNOCKED OFF HIS SOAPBOX

By DAVID HUGHES Political Editor

JOHN MAJOR suffered a first-round body blow last night as Rupert Murdoch threw his General Election weight behind Tony Blair.

A front-page article in the media mogul's Sun newspaper called the Labour leader the "breath of fresh air" Britain needs.

The tabloid's pro-Tory influence over its ten million readers has been credited with playing a big part in the Conservatives' previous election victories — in 1992, the paper claimed it was 'the Sun wot won it'.

Equally significantly, its attitude is known to reflect the personal feelings of Mr Murdoch, who controls three other national newspapers and Sky TV. Under two previous editors, the paper has backed the Tories to the hilt.

There was dismay at Conservative HQ as the Sun announcement spoiled what had been a strong first-day performance from the Prime Minister.

Back at the battlefront: Pages six and seven

Within hours of announcing a May 1 poll, he was back on the soapbox he believes helped him turn the tide in 1992, facing a noisy crowd in Luton and yelling to make himself heard.

As Tories chanted 'five more years' and hecklers answered 'five more weeks', Mr Major shouted: 'We had the same noisy demonstrators here in 1992, and the Conservatives went on to win the General Election. We will do it again.'

The confrontation delighted his aides. 'He revels in these encounters and the more he gets, the better he'll like it,' said one.

In stark contrast, Mr Blair began his push for Downing Street in a smart country house hotel in Gloucester, trying to persuade wavering Tory voters that New Labour is safe to vote for.

The Labour leader stressed the 'time for change' message that will dominate his campaign. He

Turn to Page 2, Col. 1

I'M SO RELIEVED IT'S ALL OVER, SAYS TAUNTS VICTIM

Fired with delight: Mrs Clayton after winning her compensation yesterday

Bullied firewoman awarded £200,000

By JAMES GOLDEN

ONE of Britain's first women firefighters celebrated last night after being awarded a record £200,000 for a catalogue of bullying.

Tania Clayton, 31, said male colleagues in the Hereford and Worcester brigade had victimised her over five years and called her a 'cow' and a 'tart'.

Smiling after the out-of-court settlement, she said: 'I am very relieved. It has been a long hard fight and I am still in a state of shock that it is over.'

Mrs Clayton, who needed psychiatric help after being discharged on medical grounds, added: 'I could not handle it day in, day out. The station was like an old boys' network.

'Even daily drills became an ordeal and I was physically sick with worry before getting to work.'

FULL STORY: PAGE FIVE

INSIDE: John Edwards 10, Femail 22-23, Good Health 34-42, Letters 43, TV 44-46, Coffee Break 50-52, Win A Home 53, City 55-57, Sport 58-64

TONY BLAIR, surrounded by children yesterday, spoke of his crusade for a better Britain to The Mirror – the paper that's always supported Labour.

THE **Sun**

An historic announcement from Britain's No 1 newspaper

Tuesday, March 18, 1997   28p   THE PAPER OF THE PEOPLE

THE SUN BACKS BLAIR

Give change a chance

Historic . . Blair reads early copy of today's Sun

THIS is the election for the millennium.

In six weeks' time, Britain will vote for a government to take it into the 21st century.

The people need a leader with vision, purpose and courage who can inspire them and fire their imaginations.

The Sun believes that man is Tony Blair. He is the best man for the job, for our ten million readers and for the country.

It is a momentous decision which we have not taken lightly because we still have reservations about some of New Labour's policies. But for all the Tories' achievements of the past 18 years, they no longer deserve our support.

They are tired, divided and rudderless. They need a rest and so does the country. Blair is the breath of fresh air this great country needs.

On Pages 6 and 7 we explain why we are putting our trust in him.

Election special — Pages 2, 4, 5, 6 and 7

more than a manner of constructing texts which relies on a series of shooting and recording techniques which are used with the specific intention of attempting to recreate for the audience a sense of credibility in the text.

ACTIVITY 6.3   Using representations to attract an audience

The covers of two UK magazines covers are reproduced on the following pages. To identify how the covers represent the contents of the magazine, and to help you to think about how these sets of representations were chosen to attract a particular audience, you will need to use the following guidelines:

1 Who or what is shown on each of these covers? Consider:
   ■ the proportion of print to image
   ■ who or what the images show
   ■ how many typefaces have been used
   ■ sizes and styles of typefaces
   ■ overall appearance.
2 For each cover make a list of what the images lead you to expect to find inside each magazine.
3 What does the design style lead you to expect to find inside each magazine? List why.
4 Would you buy any of these publications for yourself?
   If you would not buy one of these yourself, who might you expect to buy it?
5 Who do you think that the publishers expect or want to buy each of these magazines?
6 You may wish to take the title, price and frequency of publishing into consideration.
7 How did you reach your conclusions?

FA CUP FINAL PREVIEWED INSIDE

THE ESSENTIAL FOOTBALL MONTHLY

JUNE 1997
£2.40

goal

Solskjaer, Leboeuf, Bergkamp, Laudrup, Cantona, Ravanelli Vialli Carbone, Kinkladze, Asprilla, Juninho, **Zola...**

"I'VE ALWAYS FELT BIG ENOUGH. I'VE ALWAYS BEEN HAPPY TO BE SMALL."

EXCLUSIVE INTERVIEW

with **Chelsea's pocket genius**

The 100 Best Foreign Players in Britain

From Man Utd to Motherwell EVERY overseas footballer in the country REVIEWED and RATED

JUNE 1997

The representations used on the covers of print publications are the first point of contact between the text and its potential consumers and are carefully targeted, as the previous exercise will have shown. Covers fulfil the same function as film posters, record, CD and video covers and the continuity, pre-title and title sequences used by the broadcast media.

Although audiences may have some prior knowledge of a text through advance marketing, or through their pre-existing knowledge of the series, writer, or director (depending on the medium), they make their final decision when they are confronted with the text itself. How the text represents its contents at this point is therefore vital to the decision made by each member of the audience. If the first contact with a text represents nothing of interest, then the text is likely to be passed over by the individual for something that does engage immediate interest. One obvious effect of the selection of these front-cover images is therefore, how they affect the purchasing decisions and further circulation of the text itself. There is a direct relationship between how the cover represents the contents and how this representation affects the financial success or failure of the product.

Some texts are relaunched and repackaged from time to time, without the actual contents or text having been changed at all. This is quite common in the paperback publishing industry, where books are often reissued with new cover images. For example, when a film or a television series is made of a novel, a new edition of the novel may be published using a cover image from the film.

ACTIVITY 6.4   Selling the same material again

1 Describe the images on each of the covers of *1984* on page 80.
2 What does the image on each cover suggest to you that the story might be about?
3 How might these covers attract different audiences?
4 How much is the target audience reflected in the representations on the covers?

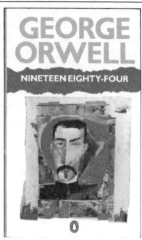

Stereotyping

We hear a lot about stereotyping and the effects on those who are portrayed by stereotypes. What is not always made clear is what is meant by stereotyping and how we can judge when a representation is stereotypical and when it is not.

In order to gain a full understanding of the word 'stereotype' it is necessary to consider its origins. A stereotype was originally the name of a printer's metal plate which was used as an original from which to print exact copies. In this definition lies the basis of the modern political use of the word, for when we talk about people being stereotyped by the media we mean that an assumption has been made that people are the same as each other, rather than individuals.

There are many examples of groups who have been stereotyped in the media. You may be a member of one of these groups yourself, for example a football supporter, a teenager, a member of a minority ethnic group or an environmental activist. The power of stereotyping may have been revealed to you as you read the previous sentence. If images floated in your mind about the appearance or character of the members of the groups mentioned, the chances are they were stereotypical images which came complete with value-judgements and a personal opinion. It may be that you know people who are members of such groups, or that as a member of some or all of them yourself, you might be wondering why some of the images you carry of the 'otherness' of such groups are not images that you might apply wholly to yourself or to people you know.

The answer, of course, lies in the uses and function of stereotyping. Stereotyped images and language are used by society and the media as a kind of cultural short-cut. By referring to a few simple descriptors, it is possible to invoke for an audience a 'type' of person about whom the audience might have pre-existing knowledge. The more often social stereotypes are referred to or invoked, the more quickly audiences will understand what they are meant to be referencing from their store of pre-existing knowledge. For example, the following list might make you think of a particular group of people:

- boots
- guns
- hat
- America
- horse
- nineteenth century

You have probably thought of cowboys. From a short list of words you have referenced the usual representation of a group of people who were instrumental in building the largest democracy in the world. Yet there is no room in this list for the concept of an individual cowboy. By stereotyping, it is possible to reduce all the individuals to the point where they can be recognised as members of a larger group by the use of an extremely simple set of reference points. It may be true that many 'cowboys' held some or all of the things on the list in common; but it is certainly true that every cowboy was an individual human being with his own characteristics. The simple reduction to a list of possible common denominators adds nothing to our understanding of either the individuals or of the group as a whole. This remains true whether the representation is part of a fiction, news or documentary text.

Stereotyping is an invitation to accept this general and limited picture of a group, and the assumption is that audiences will not question why stereotypes are thus limited. Media producers would probably say that production conditions, financial constraints or particular narratives sometimes demand that some people or characters are drawn only with the broadest of strokes; that it is enough in some cases to give the audience a general idea of a character. This argument may be just about acceptable for fiction, for example when an adaptation of a nineteenth-century English novel forms the basis of the media text, but the use of stereotyping in contemporary drama, news or documentary material in any medium raises important issues which must be explored.

Stereotyping is a form of representation which works on actual or assumed commonalities among individuals; news representations of minority or non-mainstream groups often use stereotypes. A set of easily recognised descriptors of, for example, environmental activists may be used across the news media to offer a view of this group as disruptive, dirty, left-wing, causing expense to authorities and preventing the vital work of building much-needed roads. If there is a danger in the use of stereotyping, it is that members of the audience who gather all their information about the roads debate from mainstream media may find that all the information offered expresses the same viewpoint. Access to other viewpoints may be difficult to obtain for the general public, and as a result some people may simply accept the mainstream view without questioning the representations contained within it. It may well be that many of the environmentalists do conform to the stereotype, but there are many others whose lives are lived wholly within the mainstream, but who have a particular interest in issues of environmental concern.

When employing stereotypes, mainstream media producers assume that the audiences' attitudes and values are those of the mainstream. Stereotyping is part of the naturalisation of what are offered to us as commonly held attitudes and values.

Further discussion of representations and stereotyping is included in the chapters on narrative and audience.

7 | AUDIENCE

Traditional audiences

It is important to have a clear understanding of the term 'audience' both in its accepted sense and in the specific sense in which it is used in media studies. In normal usage we apply the term to any assembled group attending an audio-visual performance. The members of the audience have a simultaneous, joint experience of the event. Such events usually take place in specially constructed auditoria, often in low lighting or darkness and the emphasis is on a seated audience listening to, hearing or watching the event while being quiet themselves. Drama, opera, music and film are exhibited in public auditoria and there are certain social conventions which are associated with 'being a member of the audience' for these events. For example, many people attend the opera or the theatre in evening dress. A distinction is often made when describing the people attending sports events, who are usually described as spectators or crowds rather than as audiences. The emphasis at these events is on watching rather than on listening and the social conventions of being a spectator demand less formal behaviour than those of being a member of an audience.

Media audiences

It might seem strange, then, that the word 'audience' has been adopted within media studies to describe the consumers of a wide range of mass-media texts which are received and consumed in a number of different contexts. At first glance it seems that only the consumption of film at the cinema neatly fits the criteria for the traditional definition of audience. Newspapers, magazines and comics, which are consumed visually by individuals, are also said by media students to have audiences. The mainly visual media of television, video and computer programmes have audiences which can vary in size from an individual to groups. Records, tapes, CDs and radio may also be heard and consumed by individuals or groups. Media consumption may be in public or private spaces, and can be domestic, leisure or work related. The variations in the contexts in which media consumption takes place are innumerable. Sometimes texts may be consumed in ways which change or challenge our usual methods of consumption. For example, a television current-affairs programme which includes a review of 'tomorrow's news' and which screens the front pages of the early editions of the newspapers confuses the distinction between television and newspaper audiences, and changes the usual context of newspaper consumption from an individual to a group activity. The use of the term 'audience' about consumers of the mass media cannot have the rigid meaning of the traditional definition of the term.

Key differences

There are some key differences between traditional audiences and media audiences:

- Mass-media audiences do not have to assemble to consume a text.
- Even one individual watching television can constitute a media audience.

Due to the ways in which media texts are produced and circulated, audiences can choose to consume the mass media in a broad range of settings. This is true in the case of the print media, where texts have always been portable and access requires no additional technology. The multiple production of electronic media texts and the introduction of domestic hardware has extended this availability to other forms.

Mass-media audiences do not have to consume a text at the same time as each other. There are, of course, times when this does occur, but an audience of 20 million for live broadcast of a programme, might be in as many different places. Some of them may not be watching the live broadcast of a programme but may be watching in different time zones or time-shifting their viewing by using a video recorder. Whether or not consumption is simultaneous, everybody who has seen, heard or read a text is considered to be part of the audience for that text.

Media audiences do not need to have chosen to participate as members of an audience to consume a particular text. If we want to go to the opera we must buy a ticket and go to the opera house. Yet we often consume mass-media texts involuntarily and without paying. Some texts are themselves for sale, while others are produced with the specific intention of free circulation. When you catch a bus you will probably see advertisements while you are on the way to the bus-stop, hear music played on car radios or stereos while you wait and might read the headlines on somebody else's newspaper while you travel.

Media audiences can have control over the conditions in which they consume texts. If people choose not to attend public exhibitions, they can watch a film or video in bed, listen to music in the bathtub or do the ironing while they watch television. The social conventions associated with public auditoria do not apply to the private or domestic consumption of texts.

Domestic media audiences have greater control over how much of a text they consume. At a public screening of a film, for example, the individual's choice of how much of the text to consume usually extends to watching the whole text, falling asleep or leaving the auditorium. Domestic consumption allows a far greater range of response because we own, or at least hire, the technology and the texts. Consumption at home is usually cheaper than attending public events, and the experience of home consumption is very different. We might choose to watch part of a programme, read a few pages of a play, listen to three tracks from an album and either return to the text later, or not at all.

Domestic audiences can choose what to do with a text after they have consumed it. Private ownership or hire of media texts allows individuals to make decisions about what happens to a text. Newspapers and magazines are used for a variety of purposes, from lining the cat's tray to having parts selected and kept as cuttings on walls or in scrapbooks. CDs, tapes and videos are copied, edited, used to make new compilations, taped over or lent to others. That is to say that copies of some texts become consumable as physical objects as well as for their contents. The texts themselves are not necessarily durable, or even designed to be, though they may be treated as such.

Media audiences can make their own texts and circulate them. Not only can we modify texts made by other people, but we can also originate our own texts. Until comparatively recently high-quality and easy-to-operate media hardware, other than still or cine cameras and simple tape recorders, was not available to the general public. Since the development of the cheap micro-chip it has become possible for many more people to become media producers. What we produce varies from the purely amateur text designed for family consumption to texts which are circulated much more widely, for example alternative print or video newspapers and home-produced music tapes or CDs.

ACTIVITY 7.1 Media log

Log your media consumption for one day. Choose whichever day of the week is easiest for you to record. Remember that your choice of day will influence the conclusions you draw at the end of the exercise.

Your chart should look like this:

Time	Medium	Place	Vol./Invol.

Fill in the boxes for each 30-minute block for one day, from waking to going to sleep. Include everything you can.

You may be surprised to realise how much time you spend in one day consuming media, that is, how often you were a member of a media audience.

1 Which of your involvements with media texts were:
   a) voluntary?
   b) involuntary?
2 Which did you pay for:
   a) directly?
   b) indirectly?
   c) not at all that you are aware of?

The last two parts of question 2 (above) are difficult to answer. The distinction between voluntary and involuntary consumption is not easy to draw. You may have glanced involuntarily at a street hoarding, then become intrigued by the advertisement and carried on looking at or thinking about the poster voluntarily. You may have been doing the washing-up with the radio playing, not listening consciously, and suddenly had your attention seized by a news bulletin to which you then listened attentively.

It can also be difficult to be certain about the distinction between purchased and free texts. We may buy newspapers, but we also read other people's. Advertising hoardings are free to look at, but marketing costs are included in the purchase price of the goods in the shops. Public service broadcasting is funded through the licence fee in Britain, but commercial stations are not paid for in this way by audiences. You may feel that you have thought of some texts which are completely free to the consumer but these cover all their production, marketing and circulation costs by adjusting the final purchase price of their goods, so think about where the hidden costs lie and who pays for them.

Membership of media audiences

With so much to choose from it is useful to think about how individuals become members of the audience for a particular text. Our common-sense assumption is that we choose to participate as audience, yet we also know from keeping a media diary that we sometimes consume media texts involuntarily, one might say accidentally. It is, however, true to say that being a member of an audience is mostly a matter of choice. So how do we choose?

We do not make choices without help or influence. Try to remember your earliest media experiences, possibly your favourite childhood television programmes. You did not choose them yourself: adults selected them for you from what was available and chose what they believed to be suitable for a young child. You might now be wondering what criteria were used when people made these choices for you. Adults may have based their judgement on their own preferred programmes, on listings or reviews in newspapers and magazines or on conversations held with other people bringing up young children.

As children grow older they begin to *request* some programmes and to reject others, to watch some programmes all the way through or to turn to their toys when they find the programme uninteresting. They begin to develop some preferences of their own, based on their limited experience of television. They may also find themselves in the position of having the channel changed, or the television turned off if an adult considers that the broadcast is unsuitable for children. This is a common experience. Although the *content* of texts considered suitable or unsuitable for young people may vary as social practice changes, for at least the first few years of a child's life adults take the responsibility of selecting media for them. In this way preferences set by early media consumption can influence later choices.

As children grow older they extend their media consumption. They consume more media in a broader range of contexts: at home, at school and in public places. The patterns of planned and accidental media consumption are set early in our lives. Photographs are taken and family albums established and young children begin to recognise themselves and relatives from these. The first written words that children see regularly are often on food packaging, sweet wrappers, advertisements and, more recently, video-tape covers. Young children become aware of music, radio, newspapers, magazines in the home and later begin to own media texts such as videos, comics and books. Children repeatedly choose their favourite stories or programmes which they consume alongside texts which are new to them. Children begin to visit the cinema. At school they begin to experience more formal and directed uses of the media, which adds a new dimension to their existing uses for leisure or entertainment purposes. Children may receive cameras, televisions, music centres, video recorders and computers as they grow older, and use these media at school and at home in different ways, for different purposes and from different motivations.

However, domestic and social uses of the media continue to differ from educational or work-related uses for most people. In the private context, we use different criteria to choose what we consume and what we produce.

ACTIVITY 7.2   Criteria for choice

It is useful at this point to think in a little more detail about why you watch certain programmes. This activity is designed to help you beyond simply knowing *what* you watch and to encourage more structured thought about *why* you watch.

Start by identifying two television programmes:

■ Your favourite drama, soap or comedy programme.
■ A news, current affairs or documentary programme you watch most often.

Answer the questions which follow to help you to structure your thinking:

Drama, soap or comedy:

1 Who is your favourite character?

2 What do you like about her/him?

3 Who is your least favourite character?

4 What do you dislike about her/him?

5 In what kind of situations do the characters find themselves?

6 Do people's opinions differ about how the characters should behave?

7 Have you experienced any similar situations in real life?

8 What *pleasure* do you experience when watching this programme?

9 Do you ever have any pleasure after or between episodes?

10 Do you ever read about the programme in magazines or newspapers?

11 Why do you continue to watch it?

12 What would happen if you stopped?

News, current affairs or documentary:

1 How would you describe the kind of programme you have chosen?

2 Do you regard the programme as informative?

3 Do you ever think about checking the information that's given?

4 Do you regard the programme as entertaining?

5 Do you usually agree with the programme-maker's point of view?

6 How often do you discuss the programme with others?

7 Describe the presenter(s), if they are shown on-screen.

8 What do you like about the presenter(s)?

9 If you dislike the presenter(s), why do you still watch the programme?

10 What pleasure do you get from watching this programme?

Common to both types of programme:

1 How often is the programme broadcast?

2 How long does it last?

3 At what time(s) in the week is it broadcast?

4 Do you know which company makes the programme?

5 Do other people in your household watch it?

6 Do you always watch it at home?

7 If you are away from home do you watch it anyway, or make arrangements to catch up in another way?

8 Do your friends watch the programme?

9 Do you ever discuss the programme with friends or family?

10 How did you hear about the programme?

11 What encouraged you to watch the programme the first time?

12 Can you hum or sing the theme tune?

13 Do you ever put off doing something else to watch this programme?

14 If not, do you time-shift your viewing by using the video recorder?

15 Do you ever do anything else while 'watching' the programme?

16 If so, what do you do?

Conclusions

Look back at your notes. You should now know more about how and why you make certain viewing choices; perhaps enough to conclude that you use different programmes in different ways and that your pleasures vary. You may have discovered that there is more to viewing pleasure than the obvious. Enjoying watching a narrative unfold or laughing at something that is humourous are easily identified pleasures. Looking forward to a broadcast or discussing it afterwards, arguing with friends about the outcome or disagreeing with newspapers' critics are not always thought of as pleasures derived from the text itself, but they are some of the pleasures of being in an audience.

In doing this exercise, you may have thought of more questions to ask yourself about specific areas of media consumption. Try the exercise again using, for example, a commercial radio programme or a film, and make an extended list of points to think about, using the questions on the existing chart as a guide.

Texts are products

You are aware that media texts are products and that, like other products, they are sold. This aspect of the media as producers of consumer commodities is key to reaching an understanding of how individuals become part of the audience for any given text. If there were no audience to receive the text at the end of the production process texts would not be produced and media hardware would not be manufactured. The audience is the most vital part of the economics of the media industries and the choices made by individuals ultimately influence production processes and the circulation of texts. The organisation of media industries and institutions is discussed in more detail elsewhere in this book, but there are certain aspects of industrial practice which are relevant to the present study of audience. Producers and marketing departments in the media industries wish to ensure that their products sell to the public and use a wide variety of methods in attempts to achieve this. Some of these strategies are common across the media whereas others are specific to individual media forms.

Reaching audiences

Constructing audiences

The audience is the market for media texts. Whether the production is a text which will be on sale direct to the public, for example a magazine, or a text whose function is to sell another product, such as an advertisement for a new chocolate bar, the relationship between the audience and the text is the same. The basis of this relationship is that each member of the public must see him or herself as a member of an audience. In some senses every one of us is part of an audience nearly all the time, but to move from the relatively passive position of receiver to that of active consumer, we must become willing to participate in our own audiencehood. That is, we must actively include ourselves in the process of making sense of texts, of decoding them and of making meanings from them. Most people will choose to do this only at certain times for texts which they know, or have come to believe will interest them. The skill of constructing an audience lies in making people believe and accept that certain texts have been produced especially for them, or at least for people like them.

Targeting and segmenting audiences

In media studies' terms, audiences are 'targeted' by producers to encourage them to become consumers for certain texts. Texts are targeted at certain social groups or audiences. The practice of targeting audiences is an attempt to break down the idea that the population is a mass and to think instead of 'segments' of people within the population. The intention is to reach specific parts or groups of people. The existence of various groups within our society has been established by research into all aspects of our lives. Sometimes media institutions carry out this research themselves, as when a television company commissions a breakdown of accommodation, income rates and types of employment within the region to which it broadcasts. Much of the information is gathered by central government departments, and research produced by non-government organisations and universities can be of use to media institutions when identifying and segmenting audiences.

A media industry which makes particular use of this idea of segmenting audiences is the advertising industry. For example, advertisers in the UK use the following social and economic gradings as a method of dividing the population according to notional spending power. These grades are used when targeting audiences for products:

- **A** higher management/professional
- **B** middle management/administration/professional
- **C1** junior management/supervisory/professional
- **C2** skilled manual
- **D** semi-skilled/unskilled manual
- **E** unemployed/casual workers/pensioners

Another way to think of audience segments is to consider how people see themselves, rather than to look only at their economic or social position. Such groupings include:

Succeeders	think of themselves as powerful and in control
Aspirers	want a better life
Carers	have a social conscience
Mainstreamers	prefer to be like most other people
Individualists	prefer to be different from most other people

Some media theorists believe that it is individuals' membership of existing social groups which causes them to prefer some texts to others.

John Hartley (*Understanding News*, 1982) defined the factors that create these social groups as based on:

- self
- gender
- age group
- family
- class
- nation and ethnicity.

In a later work (*Television Culture*, 1987) John Fiske added the following to the list of factors which can contribute to the social position of individuals:

- education
- religion
- political allegiance
- region
- urban or rural background.

You will have noticed that membership of some of these groups is outside the control of the individual, whereas others can be a matter of choice. It is also possible for people to move between groups at different times in their lives, for instance by revising their political opinions or changing religion. Just as audiences are not fixed, neither are the factors which are often used to define them.

It is unlikely that audiences are formed entirely on the basis of the social groupings to which individuals belong. Other factors must be taken into consideration. Hobby or other interest groups tend to cut across social and economic groupings, and membership of these groups is not necessarily based on belonging to any of the categories listed above. An example of this is the market for computer magazines, whose readers may be particularly interested in some *parts* of the publication for a specific purpose, but who become nevertheless members of the audience segment for computer magazines. Thus a targeted audience can be thought of as consisting of possibly disparate individuals who temporarily form an homogenous group. Some members of the computer-magazine audience may be occasional purchasers, or might not be loyal to a particular publication from week to week.

Some people are regular consumers of particular texts or products, for example magazine subscribers or people who follow serials on the radio or television. In this case audiences are defined by those texts, as in 'the *Cheers* audience', or 'the *National Geographic* audience'. For some people this product loyalty is connected to characters, performers and personalities, and loyalty increases to include texts produced in other media forms and any merchandise which is connected to the original text. Such extreme loyalty is usually called 'fandom', and has been the subject of detailed studies in relation to film stars and pop music.

Reaching audiences

Once a product has been made with a target audience in mind it is necessary to market the product in ways which make sure that the intended audience is *reached*. Potential audiences must be informed about the product. They must be encouraged to feel that this product is for them; that is, people are *positioned* to believe that the text is relevant to them in some way. Finally, the product must be made available at convenient times and places and at a price within their disposable income.

Producers and media institutions use various kinds of advertising. There are often examples of one medium being used to advertise the products of another and this often happens when several media companies are owned by the same organisation. For example, in Britain *The Sun* newspaper often carries items about BSkyB – both of which are owned by News International. Forthcoming films are advertised on television; new music releases are advertised in the press. Specialist magazines carry advertisements for new developments within the field of interest. Quantitative research, which is used to collect facts and figures about the size of audiences, is carried out by media institutions. Market research provides detailed knowledge of who consumes what, and enables the institutions to decide where and when to promote new products most successfully.

Listings magazines inform the public about cinema programmes and television and radio schedules. Cinemas run trailers and excerpts from new releases, display posters and photographs and sell film magazines. Television stations run continuity sequences outlining features of their schedules for one day or the season. Newspapers and magazines publish reviews, recommendations and articles about forthcoming products in the rest of the media. Record shops display posters and sales charts of the best-selling tracks. Bookshops display charts and offer discounted prices on certain books. Supermarkets, toyshops and hobby shops stock merchandise associated with some films or television programmes. Schools use reading books which are themselves spin-offs from children's television programmes. There are numerous opportunities for producers to reach audiences with information about where to find what they wish to consume.

Counting audiences

Media institutions monitor how many people consume their output. Since this is concerned with audience size, it is called 'quantitative' research. There are various joint industry committees in the UK which are responsible for researching into audience preferences and counting viewers, listeners and readers.

In the UK the Broadcasters' Audience Research Board (BARB), co-ordinates the quantitative audience research carried out by the BBC, ITV and the Joint Industry Committee for Television Audience Research (JICTAR). Quantitative research is used to count consumers and their consumption. Using a sample of 3,000 homes, researchers calculate the 'average audience' over the whole transmission, the 'core audience', that is anyone who has watched or listened to a programme all the way through and the 'programme reach' which identifies how many people have watched or listened to part of the programme. They also calculate the average daily and weekly reach for given programmes or whole stations, and the 'audience share' between broadcasting organisations. This information is collected electronically from households where it has been agreed that computerised monitoring equipment can be attached to their television. Participants also keep a diary. Results of the monitoring are published weekly in the trade press and often in the national daily newspapers in the form of charts.

Research into consumption by radio audiences is carried out by the Radio Authority and the BBC and is co-ordinated by the Joint Industry

Committee for Radio Audience Research. This information is recorded by members of the public in diaries on either a daily or weekly basis.

Other methods of monitoring include audience surveys, questionnaires, discussion groups which are organised around screenings of pilot episodes of new programmes, surveys of audience likes and dislikes and observation by media professionals of people consuming radio and television programmes. In the UK broadcasters also provide some structured opportunities on air for audience feedback in programmes like *Points of View* and *Hard News* which allow members of the public to have access to producers and the chance to comment on output. Much of this research is qualitative, rather than quantitative. In qualitative research the emphasis is on how consumers respond to various aspects of the product, for example content or how much they enjoyed the programme.

Similar processes are in operation in the UK print industries. For example, in Britain the Joint Industry Committee for National Readership Surveys (JICNARS) monitors newspaper readership and responses and the Audit Bureau of Circulation (ABC) keeps account of newspaper and magazine sales. Competition between daily newspapers is especially fierce, and the struggle to gain and retain readers has led to specific strategies within the industry. Price wars have become common, as have special offers to readers, for example free travel offers when a certain number of tokens are collected, and scratchcards. Some papers run theatre clubs, travel clubs and other membership based activities.

A number of sales charts are kept for other media products, including pre-recorded and blank video and audio tapes. Music charts are published weekly, broken into separate charts for different types of music, for example, classical, independent and popular.

The circle of targeting, distribution and research is thus complete. Figures collated from quantitative research and feedback obtained about the quality of products are used by media institutions to re-focus production, purchasing and scheduling policies and then to identify new audiences to target.

Keeping audiences

Once a media institution has attracted an audience, and people have settled in front of the television screen or bought the newspaper, the next challenge arises for the institutions. This is, how do they keep audiences consuming *their* product rather than a similar product produced by another company? Competition is keen and it is as important to keep one's own audience as it is to attract consumers away from other institutions' products. Strategies to ensure loyalty vary between institutions and media forms.

Television stations attempt to prevent viewers from changing channels by arranging schedules in the hope that it will be difficult for viewers to turn over. The pattern of a day's broadcasts reflects what a company believes to be the audience at different parts of the day and schedules are finely tuned to attract and to keep audiences. Less popular or new programmes may be scheduled immediately after popular programmes in the hope that inertia will cause the next programme to 'inherit' the audience. Less popular programmes are sometimes screened between two popular

---

ACTIVITY 7.3

An examination of two UK television schedules for one day will clarify what has been said in this chapter and will give you a chance to apply what you have learned.

Using the information which has been provided in this chapter about social groupings and grades, try to identify the target audience for each programme, or block of programmes.

	BBC 1	ITV Carlton
TIME	TITLE AUDIENCE	TITLE AUDIENCE

1 Do you see any patterns of broadcasting which emerge as the schedule unfolds?

2 How often are programmes of the same type scheduled against each other?

3 What things are broadcast but do not appear in the published schedules?

4 Can you spot any examples of 'hammocking' or 'inheritance'?

BBC 1

6.00 a.m. Business Breakfast. (S) (77731)
7.00 BBC Breakfast News. (T) (89489)
9.00 Breakfast News Extra. (T) (5895644)
9.20 Cheggers' Challenge. Chef Tony Tobin helps
to turn a postmaster's front room into a country
house restaurant. Presented by Keith Chegwin.
(S) (3714828)
9.45 Kilroy. Robert Kilroy-Silk hosts the topical
discussion show. (T) (S) (9244335)
10.25 Who'll Do the Pudding? The team prepares
a sumptuous meal comprising felafel with
hummus and green beans, Thai-style chicken
kebabs and French fruit tart. (S) (8343016)
10.45 News and Weather. (T) (6778286)
10.50 Cricket: First Test. Tony Lewis introduces the
opening session of the final day's play between
England and Australia. (S) (93480793)
12.35 Neighbours. Darren decides to make his peace
with Mal, who has his eyes on Catherine, and
the unfortunate Toadfish's lamentable romantic
reverses continue. (T) (S) (4852422)
1.00 News and Weather. (T) (59248)
1.30 Regional News and Weather. (15916793)
1.40 Cricket: First Test. Further coverage from
Edgbaston. (S) (53531373)
4.00 Popeye. (6832575) **4.10** Casper. (T) (S)
(9171538) **4.35** 50/50. (T) (S) (6147002)
5.00 Newsround. (T) (S) (8869915) **5.10** Blue
Peter. (T) (S) (7526118)
5.35 Neighbours. (R) (T) (S) (653915)
6.00 News and Weather. (T) (538)
6.30 Regional News Magazine. (118) (**N.Ireland:**
Newsline 6.30; **Wales:** Wales Today)
7.00 Big Break. Jim Davidson hosts the snooker-
based game show with guest players Alex
Higgins, Ray Reardon and David Roe potting
on behalf of their contestant partners, and John
Virgo keeping track of the scores. (T) (S) (7064)

7.30 CHOICE **Mastermind.** See Pick of the Day. (T)
(S) (642)

8.00 EastEnders. Mark makes a decision about his
future, Ted considers the high price of freedom
and Lorraine finds that certain matters are being
taken out of her hands. (T) (S) (6712)

8.30 CHOICE **The Peter Principle.** See Pick of the
Day. (T) (S) (5847)

9.00 News and Weather. (T) (4199)
9.30 Birds of a Feather. Tracey's joy at Darryl's
release from prison proves to be short-lived, and
Chris's new-found freedom proves to be a mixed
blessing for her friend Sharon. Starring Linda
Robson and Pauline Quirke. (T) (S) (55847)
10.00 Panorama. Another in-depth current affairs
report. (T) (931625)
10.40 Stephen King's It. First of a two-part
adaptation of the best-selling novel. Following
the apparently senseless murder of a young girl,
seven friends reunite to fight the supernatural
enemy they fought as children 30 years ago.
Stars Tim Curry. (R) (T) (S) (8150354)
12.10 FILM **Billy Two Hats** (1973). See Film Choice.
(331045)
1.45 - 1.50 a.m. Weather. (6872768)

ITV Carlton

6.00 a.m. GMTV. (9667731) **9.25** Supermarket
Sweep. (R) (T) (S) (3722847) **9.55** London
Today. (T) (4409880) **10.00** The Time, the
Place. (S) (21977) **10.30** This Morning. (T)
(65853460) **12.20** Your Shout. (1861606)
12.25 London Today. (T) (1860977) **12.30**
News and Weather. (T) (4888847) **12.55**
London Today. (T) (4863538)
1.25 Home and Away. Travis feels rejuvenated after
his heroic escapade. (T) (S) (90066809)
1.50 Baby Matters. (31420064) **2.20** Blue Heelers.
(S) (3960880) **3.15** Breakaways. (R) (3034731)
3.20 News Headlines. (T) (3031644) **3.25**
London Today. (T) (3030915) **3.30** Caribou
Kitchen. (3841002) **3.40** Tots TV. (R) (S)
(8797083) **3.50** Cartoon Time. (R) (3293248)
3.55 Where's Wally? (R) (T) (S) (7245847) **4.25**
Woof! (R) (9194489) **4.50** The Big Bang. (T)
(S) (4624335) **5.10** Home and Away. (R) (T)
(S) (8756712) **5.40** News and Weather. (T)
(896793) **6.00** London Tonight. (T) (606) **6.30**
London Bridge. (S) (286)
7.00 Wheel of Fortune. Game show. (T) (S) (5460)
7.30 Coronation Street. Judy decides that the time
has come to reveal all about her past. (T) (170)
8.00 World in Action. Part two of the report
investigating British links with Indonesia's
military dictatorship. (T) (S) (1880)
8.30 Turner round the World. Anthea Turner hosts
the globetrotting game show. (S) (1165)

9.00 CHOICE **Bramwell.** See Pick of the Day. (T)
(S) (8286)

10.00 News and Weather. (T) (97098)
10.30 London Tonight. (T) (382625)
10.40 Pulling Power. (T) (893880)
11.10 Something Strange. (747538) **11.40** Hunter.
(R) (325460) **12.40** War of the Worlds.
(R) (7032720) **1.35** Late and Loud. (S)
(4685316) **2.40** Real Stories of the Highway
Patrol. (2756045)
3.05 FILM **Thrill Kill** (1982). Average thriller with
Robin Ward and Gina Massey. *SB* (3100381)
4.30 Jody Horowitz Reports. (52831855) **4.35**
World in Action. (R) (T) (S) (81080652) **5.00**
The Time, the Place. (T) (S) (73300) **5.30 -**
6.00 a.m. News. (40497)

**Schoolmaster Mr Horne (Ken Bones) confides in
Eleanor Bramwell (Jemma Redgrave)** *(ITV, 9.00 pm)*

programmes, so that this 'hammock' will discourage people from changing channel for the duration of one programme only. New programmes are often screened at the beginning or end of the day's broadcast until some audience following is established, and then moved into peak hours. The most popular programmes rarely have their places in the schedules changed. In the breaks between programmes companies run trailers and continuity sequences to keep people watching, and announcers constantly remind us of what is to follow. Even dedicated satellite television channels use these strategies to keep their audiences watching.

Merchandising

Merchandising is worth separate consideration, as it is a strategy which expands many of the audience-related issues already discussed. The merchandising of goods which are linked to a particular media text or group of texts has become a lucrative part of the economy of media institutions. The Disney Corporation is perhaps the best-known example of a company which produces a range of items, not necessarily media texts, which can be purchased by actual or potential viewers of many of the Corporation's films. Recent examples of films which have been promoted in this way include *Pocahontas* and *The Hunchback of Notre Dame*. The range of goods associated with the film texts is impressive, including toys, mugs, games, clothing and even reproduction animation cells. The goods are circulated through toy and gift shops, through Disney outlets on the high street and at the Corporation's theme parks.

Merchandising is a growing segment of the media economy and an increasing number of texts now have a range of products associated with them. In 1996 the success of the film *Trainspotting* led not only to the original novel from which the film was adapted being reprinted several times, but also to an explosion of posters, T-shirts, and other goods being available in time for Christmas. Merchandising links the functions of constructing, targeting, reaching and keeping audiences interested in the text.

Studying media audiences

We have already looked at some types of audience research which is carried out or commissioned by media producers and institutions. The results of such research are used to enhance the output of media institutions and to develop business opportunities.

There is a large body of research, which uses some of the same techniques as commercial research, but which is carried out for different purposes by academic researchers outside media institutions. These researchers may work in any one of a number of subject disciplines. It is possible to research into the media within, for example, departments of English, media, politics, communication, cultural studies, education, history or information technology. The variety of approaches which can be taken when researching media audiences is evidence of how far-reaching the consumption and uses of the mass media have become within modern society. The existence of so much academic research shows how the spread of the mass media in the twentieth century has led to a desire to understand the complexities of the media industries, and in particular of how audiences make sense of the output from the industries.

Academic and political debate has raged about the effects of the mass media in Europe since printing presses were first set up in the sixteenth century and the implications of the power of communicating an idea to many people almost simultaneously was recognised. What concerns us here, however, is to give a brief outline of the major trends in audience research since the invention of the electronic mass media. The greatest amount of research has been into film and television audiences.

Effects theory

Research carried out before the 1960s tended to focus on the possible effects of exposure to the mass media on audiences. Two assumptions were made: that the media generated harmful effects and that the audience consisted of an homogenous, passive mass which simply absorbed whatever was made available. The common-sense belief based on these assumptions was that social and moral degeneration would follow as a direct result of the mass consumption of moving images at public exhibition. This common-sense view was a direct result of how different both the form and content of mass-media products were from the limited circulation art forms which had been available previously. Mass-media texts were thought of as being of less worth than 'high' cultural forms, such as drama and opera, simply because they were mass produced, popular and gave people cheap access to more information and entertainment than ever before. Effects theory has its roots in cultural elitism and the political need to control information and, through this, people.

The first censorship law passed in England was in 1909, the result of concerns about cinemas screening unsuitable material. Within a year, a film of the world heavyweight boxing championship had been banned from exhibition on the grounds that the audience would 'become agitated'. The history of effects theory is that of attempts to repress, control or censor public access to texts. Often, censorship of the content or circulation of texts or restriction of public access are justified by a stated commitment to protect the public from material which is thought by those with social or political responsibilities to be potentially damaging to others.

By the 1920s concerns about the effects of the media, which had in earlier times been focused on moral matters, were diverted towards political issues. The perceived role of the mass media in spreading ideas, which led to social and political revolutions in both Germany and Russia during the First World War in Europe, increased academics' and politicians' concerns about the power of the mass media to influence public opinion. During the 1920s in Russia, and the 1930s in Germany, the media were controlled by the state and encouraged to produce political propaganda to sway public opinion away from ideas of political alternatives to the existing governments. The work of the members of the Frankfurt Institute for Social Research argued that media producers were able to 'inject' attitudes and beliefs directly into the minds of the mass of the population, whom they presented as powerless to ignore what they consumed. Much of this work was based in behaviourist theories of learning. Behaviourists believed that learning took place when people were exposed to stimuli, and that responses and behaviour could be conditioned by the selection of stimuli. At the time this was thought to be borne out in the populations of Soviet Russia and Nazi Germany. During the Second World War both the Allies and the Axis used censorship and propaganda to limit and control the circulation of information and to encourage social and political attitudes.

National systems of licensing and certification of media texts are the legacy of the findings of effects' researchers. In the USA, the National Motion Picture Rating System was introduced in 1968. In Britain, films for cinema exhibition and video recordings are currently subject to the following classification, with certificates being issued by the British Board of Film Censorship (BBFC):

U   Universal. Suitable for all.

PG   Parental Guidance. General viewing, but some scenes may be unsuitable for young children.

12 Suitable only for persons of 12 years and over. Not to be supplied to any person below that age.

15 Suitable only for persons of 15 years and over. Not to be supplied to any person below that age.

18 Suitable only for persons of 18 years and over. Not to be supplied to any person below that age.

Terrestrial broadcasters in the UK are obliged to operate a 'watershed', which prevents the broadcasting before 9.00 p.m. of material which is thought unsuitable for children. Regulations operate about the display of 'adult' magazines in shops, and warnings about explicit language now appear on record, tape and CD packaging. There is a voluntary scheme for the licensing of video covers, operated by the Video Packaging Review Committee. These measures are designed to make the public aware of the contents of specific texts and to protect them from certain types of language and images.

Despite these provisions, many people still believe that legislation is not adequate, and some groups claim the right to protect audiences, especially young audiences, from material which they think is unsuitable or likely to have a detrimental effect. Such groups have a great deal of social and moral power, and are often successful at lobbying for the restriction of certain media products or changes in the law. Their activities sometimes generate what have become known among media students as 'moral panics'. These moral panics are characterised by widespread complaint and publicity targeted at texts which are thought unsuitable, and often target media producers as the cause of rising crime rates and changes in social behaviour among young people.

Opinion leaders and two-step flow

New ideas about audiences developed after the Second World War, when research carried out in America showed that effects on audiences had previously been assumed, not proven. Work by Merton (*Mass Persuasion*, 1946), Lazarsfeld (*The People's Choice*, 1944) and Katz and Lazarsfeld (*Personal Influence*, 1955) covered new ground. Their research showed that the idea of a large, indistinguishable mass of passive recipients was inaccurate, and that individuals were as likely to be influenced by their own situations or by other people's opinions as by the content of the media message. The concept of 'opinion leaders' was developed as research began to reveal that discussion among audience members could lead to a general acceptance of the opinions of the most powerful individuals in the group. It was also discovered that people who had never seen a text, for example the news, would still hold an opinion about issues covered when other people told them about the content. This was called 'two-step flow' and was taken to prove that the content of media texts alone was not responsible for forming people's attitudes.

Other research carried out during this period revealed that audiences were quite selective about choosing the texts which they consumed. For example people did not buy newspapers with whose political standpoint they disagreed. This discovery about 'selective exposure' called into question the idea that opinions could be changed by exposure to the media, by showing that audiences controlled what they consumed. Furthermore, audiences were shown to be exercising 'selective perception'; that is, they ignored opinions with which they did not already agree.

Uses and gratifications

By the 1970s the emphasis was moving away from the possible effects that the media might have on audiences and towards an investigation of what audiences *do* with the contents of the texts they consume. Research by Jay Blumler and studies by Denis McQuail (see Further Reading) placed the emphasis on how audience members processed the texts which they experienced. These researchers established the range and variety of response among audience members, which showed that the media functioned in different ways for different people. For example, viewers might use texts in a number of ways:

- as a diversion from everyday life
- to gain information about the outside world
- to compare themselves with the people represented in the media
- for company.

Audiences were found to take pleasure from the media as their needs were met and to select texts which would meet these needs, either consciously or unconsciously. The 'uses and gratifications' theory not only challenged the traditional effects' theories of audience, but also led to further research which sought to establish exactly *how* audiences extracted information from media texts.

Reception theory

More recent theories are based on the concept of audiences as individuals who each actively make sense of texts. The work carried out by Stuart Hall in the 1980s (see Further Reading) concentrated on how audiences *decoded* the information contained in media texts. His work was based on earlier theories of semiotics, and he established that an individual's ability to *decode* was based on what they brought to the reading of the text. He suggested that an individual's social class and political beliefs influence the response to any given text, regardless of what the producers have *encoded* into the text. The individual's personal context influences whether she or he accepts information as it is offered, that is, accepts 'dominant' reading; whether she or he accepts only part of the information, that is, 'negotiates' with the text; or refuses to accept what is being said and therefore 'opposes' the text. Hall's work is important because it extended the 'uses and gratifications' theory, added a political dimension to the understanding of audiences and itself became the basis of further research into how audiences received texts.

Later, Dorothy Hobson investigated audiences in *Crossroads – The Drama of a Soap Opera* (1982), and David Morley, in his books *The Nationwide Audience* (1982) and *Family Television* (1986) (see Further Reading), reported on the conditions in which people watched television as well as how they understood and made use of what they saw. This work on 'conditions of reception' offered new insights into domestic consumption of television and revealed for example how seating arrangements, possession of the remote control and secondary, and even tertiary activities going on in the room could affect audience attention and response to broadcasts.

Conclusion

Academic audience research has moved considerably since the early days of moral and political panic. Emphasis now lies on analysing the structure and messages contained within media texts. How people make sense of media messages, whether they accept the content of the messages they receive and how their active participation in creating and recreating meanings could change the text are of current concern. Research now concentrates on the idea of the 'open text' where readers bring the whole meaning to the text and on the concept of the 'supertext' which locates any given media text in the context of all others.

8 | TELEVISION PRODUCTION – CASE STUDIES

Introduction

An increasing amount of the television we view is made by independent production companies. In fact in the UK two of the channels of terrestrial television have little or no production facilities – Channels 4 and 5. Approximately one-third of the output of the BBC is now bought from other sources overseas or from independent production companies in the UK.

The BBC introduced the concept of 'producer's choice' in the early 1990s. The idea was that BBC producers of programmes would have a choice of using the BBC production resources or the outside agencies. The production resources of the BBC were divided into resource centres and were required to compete on price with external agencies. The purpose behind this was to reduce the costs of production.

Many people assume that there is a large amount of money to be made in producing television programmes. At 1997 prices Channel 4 pays £12,000 ($19,000 US) to £22,000 ($35,000 US) per half hour of programming; Channel 5 pays £10,000 ($16,000 US) to £15,000 ($24,000 US) for daytime rising to £30,000 ($48,000 US) to £50,000 ($80,000 US) for prime-time television; BBC1 and ITV can pay up to £100,000 ($160,000 US) for half an hour of factual entertainment. The cost of drama productions can increase considerably beyond this. Often these programmes become co-productions with overseas companies sharing the costs by obtaining distribution rights in their countries.

Cable and satellite stations working on considerably tighter budgets do not have the financial resources to pay these rates. An average half-hour programme on cable would be paid at £2,000 ($3,000 US) to £4,000 ($6,000 US); with satellite the sum paid may be between £5,000 ($8,000 US) to £10,000 ($16,000 US) per half hour. To give a particular example, *Can't Cook, Won't Cook* – a BBC1 daytime programme – has a budget of

£10,000 ($16,000 US) to £15,000 ($24,000 US). (Sources of financial data are from various trade magazines including *Televisual & Post Update*.)

To maximise the return from making television programmes, many production companies rely on their programmes being shown throughout the world. At festivals such as Montreux distributors sell their programme catalogues to buyers from all over the world. While little money is to be made selling to television stations in the developing world and on small cable and satellite stations, if a programme is shown widely enough the returns are sufficient to give the programme makers a return for their efforts.

As you travel around the world it becomes evident that the television 'Global Village' envisaged by Marshall McLuhan in his writings (*Understanding the Media*, 1964 – see Further Reading) is now a reality. *Neighbours* is shown in more than 60 countries worldwide; for example, in Kenya it is the most popular television programme. *Sesame Street* from the Children's Television Workshop in New York is carried in 96 countries. In Nigeria in 1992 the Nigerian Television Authority was showing the British programmes *Howard's Way*, *Bergerac*, *Ivanhoe*, *Brush Strokes*, *Horizon*, *'Allo 'Allo*, *QED*, *Duchess of Duke Street*, *Cat's Eyes*, *Expedition to the Animal Kingdom* and also *World Wide Wrestling* (the most popular programme).

The advent of satellite television has had a similarly major impact on viewing throughout the world so that, for example, SKY, Eurosport, CNN, BBC Worldwide and Discovery are available in most countries.

UK case study by Steve Miller

The case study concerns a series of three broadcast television programmes that I am producing as an independent producer. The programmes are in the final stages of production at the time of writing. The case study is presented as an example of the stages involved.

The series of three programmes are documentaries based in Kenya. The initial idea came while visiting the coast on holiday in July 1995. I was recommended to visit a private game sanctuary, Chem Chem, which was in the process of being established. The small sanctuary had obtained two rhinos and had a range of other game including zebra, buffalo and ostrich. The site of Chem Chem was idyllic, on a hill overlooking a lake. Visitors walked or rode a camel on safari through the other animals. The owner, Marcus Russell, is a charismatic character who talked enthusiastically about the project, about animal conservation and of his exploits against poaching as an honorary game warden for Kenya Wildlife Service. I left thinking that this would make an excellent documentary.

I revisited Marcus one year later in July 1996. Circumstances had changed dramatically. The rhino had been moved from Chem Chem because word had come to Marcus that a group of poaching shiftas (bandits) were planning to visit. A rhino horn is of great value (up to $40,000 US) and the gang would arrive in large numbers with automatic weapons, shooting everything in sight. The rhino had, therefore, been moved at short notice to another private game sanctuary, Lewa Downs. In addition, half of the camels had been poisoned and killed. Despite considerable help offered to the local community, numerous problems existed in local politics. It was clear that the future of Chem Chem was limited. This twist to the story made my determination to shoot a documentary stronger, as now the story of Marcus and Chem Chem became even more interesting. Research was undertaken at this stage to obtain relevant documentation from Mr Russell in Kenya.

On my return to England I approached an experienced director, Peter Sykes, with the story. He immediately accepted on the basis of profit sharing on the project. The next three months involved much of the process of pre-production. In discussion with Peter we developed an outline for a programme. This involved first-hand research. By contacting the charitable trust with which Marcus was involved – TUSK – I gained useful contacts. Library research included a detailed visit to 'Tourism Concern', a specialist organisation and library which had a considerable range of information on Kenya.

The concept of the programme was now developed, based on the impact of tourism on the wildlife in Kenya, with a specific interest in Marcus Russell and the problems he encountered at Chem Chem.

Peter, the director, and I then contacted a local production company, Cine Wessex in Winchester. The owner, David Bowerman, and his son Chris were keen on the experience of working in Kenya and hence a good fee was agreed.

Meanwhile, Marcus Russell was engaged as a consultant in Kenya to set up a programme of visits in the country using his local knowledge and contacts. Numerous faxes produced a detailed itinerary which involved considerable travel throughout the country.

Prior to leaving for Kenya I decided to film a TUSK lecture at the Royal Geographical Society. The talk was by Tony Fitzjohn who worked with George Adamson (of the film *Born Free* fame) and who is now running a game reserve in Tanzania. The evening was to be introduced by Ali McGraw (the actress whose credits include *Love Story*), and Virgina McKenna (who played Joy Adamson in *Born Free*) was also attending. These three people were all interviewed together with other interested people on the concept of eco-tourism and animal conservation in Kenya.

In order to film in Kenya, a filming licence is required from the Kenyan government. A specialist Kenyan company was employed, Viewfinders, who arranged the licence and employed a handling agent to arrange customs' clearance in Kenya. The government assigned a Liaison Officer to accompany us throughout the filming and required a synopsis of the film beforehand, a list of equipment to be imported and details of all the crew. The director and myself flew to Kenya in early December and were met by Viewfinders who took us through immigration and customs. Here we met Marcus Russell who had arrived with the two vehicles we were using – a large four-wheel drive and a safari van. Both had Kenyan drivers and short-wave radios in case of breakdowns or security problems. Marcus also served as security carrying a large handgun!

In the five days before the crew and equipment arrived Peter and I spent the time on location research, meeting people and seeing locations. Without the services of a resident, Marcus Russell, this could not have been achieved so quickly.

The crew arrived and were met by Viewfinders and transported to our first location a three-hour drive north of Nairobi. Filming started that afternoon and continued for the next two weeks at a hectic pace. We travelled extensively in our two vehicles, also by small plane, including one trip with five of us plus a full shooting kit, weighing the equivalent of one more person, in a four-seater plane!

The logistics of moving a crew including producer, director, cameraman, soundman, liaison officer, Kenya Adviser, and two drivers made for some interesting problems. All became involved in aspects of the production, for example the drivers holding the reflector screens to improve the lighting in the strong Kenyan sun.

The material was shot on Beta SP tape on a relatively old but very reliable Sony BVP70 camera which provides the quality required for broadcast television, although increasingly cheaper digital equipment is replacing it for many applications.

We had established a programme of locations and the synopsis of a programme before leaving the UK, but it became clear that the material we were gathering was developing beyond the original concept. In particular it was evident that the story of Chem Chem was moving onwards. Marcus Russell had recently accepted a new job at Lake Naivasha to set up a new game reserve – the story was changing. We used the opportunity to grab any relevant material possible. On returning to England we had 26 Beta tapes with approximately 12 hours of material recorded.

Occasional opportunities arose which we could not predict, for example standing 10 feet in the open ground in front of a group of elephants while they ate, and the same distance in front of the two rhinos that Marcus had once owned, now living in the wild, while he talked to them and they clearly recognised him. Another opportunity was to film Kuki Gallman (whose autobiography *I Dreamed of Africa* is currently being made into a Hollywood movie) at her education centre.

Peter and I viewed the tape and realised that there was a problem in that the material we had collected was for two programmes – one on Marcus Russell and the other on the human–animal conflict in Kenya. However, neither programme could be readily edited into the one-hour documentary we were anticipating and more shooting was required.

We approached a London-based distributor of documentaries who sells his products throughout the world. He expressed interest in the programme idea.

In all, in Kenya we had interview material with 18 different people – some of the interviews were long, including one with Dr David Weston, the Head of Kenya Wildlife Service, which lasted 35 minutes! All the interviews were now transcribed from audio tape on to hard copy and ran to 115 pages of type. This was necessary to identify the key parts of the interviews to edit.

We decided to film additional material on Marcus who by now had developed the game reserve at Kongoni at Lake Naivasha. After some planning the timing of the visit was dictated by the need to move six rhinos from one reserve that specialised in breeding them to Kongoni. Again I booked a Betacam shooting kit, with a Sony BVW 400 camera. Because of the nature of the filming on this occasion I went as producer/director with only a cameraman, Rob Emmanuel. This gave us the considerable flexibility of moving quickly without a large crew to get in the way. However, it did at times prove difficult as I had to assist the cameraman in moving and setting-up equipment and operating sound (a gun, directional microphone). Thus, when I was interviewing I was also directing and acting as soundman at the same time! This created problems as I find interviewing involves considerable concentration, and to be involved in anything technical at the same time is difficult, to say the least. Thinking ahead of what to ask, and to be aware of what the camera is doing and what the interviewee is saying requires a great deal of concentration!

The style adopted on the second filming was much closer to news gathering, unlike the first filming where it was easier to manage the situation.

At Kongoni we rushed from one situation to another without having any control over what was to happen. For example, one morning at two minutes' notice we rushed to a water tank into which a buffalo had fallen during the night. We filmed it being tranquillised and hauled out of the tank, moved into the reserve and given a second drug to counteract the effect of the tranquilliser and then released – a happy ending and some superb footage.

In filming, events can often be unpredictable. On our third day we filmed the rhinos being moved. The animals were darted from a helicopter and once they were tranquillised the team moved in – partially reviving the rhinos and then manoeuvring them into a crate for transportation. We arrived as the first rhino was just going down and the dart was taking effect. Rob, the cameraman, turned white and announced that the camera was not working – there was no picture in the viewfinder. He carried on filming despite this. Fortunately, the camera was working. A fault had developed because of the heat and high altitude, and the viewfinder had overheated and switched off. A one-off chance to gather very unusual material nearly turned into a disaster!

When I booked the hire of the shooting kit I was asked if we were likely to do anything dangerous. 'Only to film the capture of rhinos, partly from a helicopter', was the answer I gave. 'No problem' was the reply! However, you take enormous risks without sometimes even being conscious of it at the time, to get the shoots you want. On one occasion in late afternoon light we were filming from the open back of a pick-up truck. Driving down a steep slope we spotted a group of six lions at a distance of 12 to 20 feet from the road. As the slope of the road was steep and it was only a rough track we were moving at about five miles an hour. As we passed the lions, one dropped into a crouch position ready to jump at us. As we passed we carried on filming and only when we stopped did we realise that we were easily in leaping range and were nearly 'meals on wheels'!

To film the release of the rhinos the camera was positioned on top of the transit case. One of the animals came out very fast and looked ready to charge! To film the reserve from the air we used a four-seater plane with the door removed. The cameraman was strapped into the seat, the camera tied on to him with a climbing rope as he leaned out of the open door – all in a day's work for him.

One of the highlights of the trip, which led to some excellent footage, came from the eight-week-old cheetah cubs which were being hand-reared in the camp on the reserve. To play with cheetahs, have them purring loudly while filming them, was a real experience. Unfortunately, they were very playful and thought the camera was an exciting toy. It was interesting to have to explain to the hire company that the foam wind shield on the camera was not in very good condition because it had been chewed by a cheetah!

A shooting kit consists of a camcorder, a spare recorder, a monitor, sound kit with a gun microphone, tripod, batteries, etc. The problem of exporting this equipment by air is the considerable weight – 110 kg. Also, a fully detailed list had to be prepared and this was checked by customs on the way out so that the same equipment was declared on return. On the last trip I returned with 12 pieces of baggage in the hold of the aircraft plus my own two suitcases! The camera valued at £40,000 ($64,000 US) and the recorder at £15,000 ($24,000 US) were carried as hand baggage on to the aircraft as they are too fragile for the hold. On the return trip I also carried the tapes we shot as these were very precious.

On return to England the tapes were all copied from Beta SP to VHS with timecode in picture (this is a unique number generated by the camera which counts the sync pulses) and allows the position on the tape to be clearly identified. The tapes were then logged in detail to indicate clearly where the most useful shots were. With some 22 hours of recorded material, clearly there must be a considerable amount of unusable material – camera shake being an obvious problem when shooting from vehicles. Retakes on interviews and run-up time is also wasted tape. For editing, a period of 10 seconds is needed for the machines to lock on to the tape at the start of the sequence, so frequently the recorder is left running to ensure the run-up time.

Having logged the tape and transcribed the interviews, the next stage is a paper edit to shape the programme. From this stage, because of the huge amount of material, the tape is being initially edited on a VHS edit suite. This allows the tape to be cheaply rough cut into a programme. The material which has been selected is then digitised on to a Jazz disk to be edited on a non-linear computer editing machine. This allows great flexibility in the editing and also in the decisions about shots and sound track. The reason for editing on VHS tape first is essentially to save money. To hire edit suites costs a great deal.

Once the material has been edited on the non-linear system the shots selected from the master disk will be taken to full on-line edit suites. The computer will then control the edit suites which have reverted to using the original Beta SP tapes to make the quality master required for broadcast television. With the edit decisions now already made, a complex programme can be finished in two days.

Costings

As producer it is my responsibility to raise the finance for the programmes.

For the two-week duration shoot in 1996 the estimated costs were:

Shooting costs

flights to Kenya	£3,050
vehicle hire	£3,000
shooting equipment hire	£3,500
crew costs	£1,500
video tape	£1,000
Viewfinder in Nairobi (including filming licences)	£2,000
accommodation/food	£2,600
insurance	£300
internal flights	£400
expenses – plane/fax	£350

Post production

voice over	£400
graphics	£1,000
dubb Beta to VHS	£650
edit – non-linear, 2 weeks	£6,500
on-line edit, 2 days	£1,000
	TOTAL £27,250
	($44,000 US)

These costings are for one complete programme but the second requires one more week in Kenya and the third programme is still to be shot (a two-week shoot).

Selling

Because my company is not an established production company for broadcast television it has not been possible to obtain a commission for the programme, i.e. to persuade a broadcast company to pay up-front for the production costs.

Therefore we approached a distributor who specialises in selling documentaries in more than 80 countries. Hopefully my programmes will be sold to many channels, including cable and satellite. Each will pay a relatively small sum for every showing, but if sufficient screenings are made the programme will be profitable – the estimated costs so far do not include any fee for me as producer or for the director!

A small return was made by selling two two-minute items to the BBC children's programme *Newsround*. Although they do not credit the source of their material, this allowed the material to be shown to a wider audience, a particular request of the charity, TUSK with whom we work. Similarly, some of the material is shortly to be edited into a promotional video for TUSK, with the corporate production company CTN.

After final production is completed, surplus material will be offered to video libraries, especially the animal footage.

Conclusion

The purpose of this case study is to give some insights into the production process. In particular:

■ The role of production staff

As producer my responsibilities include raising finance, developing the idea, arranging transport and all other administration, selecting the staff and selling the programme.

The director is responsible at all stages of production from taking the programme idea and developing it into the final programme.

The camera operator is responsible to the director for the technical quality of the pictures.

■ Idea

However well planned the initial concept, in a documentary as material appears, the idea will develop. By being in the right place at the right time (a matter of planning and luck!), material will be recorded that will change the programme.

■ Planning

Preparation is critical in television production. It also takes a considerable amount of time – this production will take two years to complete. The organisation of booking crew and facilities, transport, accommodation, setting up locations and interviews, etc. are all critical to the success of filming. When working so far away from home, making the most of the time is particularly important.

■ Shooting

Documentary programme making can be 'shooting on the hoof', as was particularly the case in the second shoot. The director relies heavily on the experience and expertise of the camera operator. While a monitor is carried to view the material there is not always the opportunity or time to set it up.

Equipment breakdown is the continual worry. In a remote location there is no back-up available. With a professional camera the most likely problem is with the recorder, hence a back-up recorder is carried at all times. The heat, dust, moisture and movement across rough ground takes a toll on the equipment. Dirt on the recording head is another worrying factor. Before we left for Kenya, on each occasion the equipment was fully checked. Precautions must be taken for the safety of the equipment and crew. In our shooting we have been at considerable risk at times, but in each case, for example where we were facing wild animals, it was with expert advice available at all times.

■ Post production

Post production is very time consuming. Preparation is again the key, and the effort expended in logging tapes and transcribing interviews is very worthwhile. By keeping a shooting log at this time, considerable time can be saved in the early stages of post production.

I prefer to make a rough edit before going to an off-line on non-linear (computer) editing. This is particularly time consuming but I feel it is worthwhile as it saves money on paying for facilities and results in a refined product. The more you work with the material the more likely it is that the result will satisfy you.

Television production is expensive. The production described here is a financial risk but to gain acceptance in the industry this seems the only way to move forward. You will see from detailed costings provided, and the information in the introduction which explains how much is paid by the television broadcasters, that not all the production companies you hear of are very wealthy – it does not work like that!

US case study – *Sesame Street*

Plans for the Children's Television Workshop (CTW) started in 1967 when Joan Ganz Cooney approched the Carnegie Corporation with a proposal for a new format for pre-school television programmes. From this beginning *Sesame Street* and many other CTW programmes were created. The globalisation of *Sesame Street* has been one of the most successful of any television programme. It is currently shown in 89 countries throughout the world and it is estimated that more than 100 million children outside the United States have viewed *Sesame Street*.

The initial idea of *Sesame Street* was outlined as a 'wall-less classroom' which would seek to educate young children, using the techniques and appeal of commercial television. The programme was carefully developed to appeal to the needs of poor inner-city children as well as those of middle-class children. Before *Sesame Street*, many people thought that educational television was dull, and the United States was not highly regarded as a producer of outstanding television programmes for children. Children's television was held in low esteem and the industry had even developed the term 'Kidvid' to state its view of the genre. However, the success of *Sesame Street* and the other CTW programmes such as *The Electric Company*, *3-2-1 Contact* and *Square One TV* has changed this perception completely.

In 1968 Joan Cooney and Lloyd Marriseit, who developed the concept of *Sesame Street*, are quoted as saying that it was 'the right idea at the right time'. They targeted a number of organisations and raised $8 million to launch the first season. At the time of its launch, television was available to

97 per cent of all US households, and the civil rights movement had inspired the public to seek answers to the social and economic plight of the black minority. The 'Head Start' movement had developed a public awareness of the inequalities in educational opportunity. Within this context, *Sesame Street* must appeal to all children, both the privileged and the under privileged: and especially for the latter group, it must provide a rich learning experience and develop those school-related skills that are less available to them than the children from a middle-class, more affluent background).

In the late 1960s, research into television was coming to the forefront in academic circles. The rule and influence of television was being widely researched and was part of a widespread public debate. As the ownership of television sets had grown over the last 20 years from 10 per cent to 90 per cent the effects of television were becoming an important issue. In 1969, public broadcasting started in the United States and for the first time gave the possibilities for national exposure. It was within this context that *Sesame Street* was launched on 10 November 1969.

There was considerable press interest in the programme's launch. On 5 November 1970 the *New York Times* published an article by Andrew H Malcolm entitled 'Sesame Street Rate Excellent: 2 Year Study Finds it Helped Children of the Poor Learn'. Details from the article reported that the programme uses 'fast paced advertising techniques to instruct children in basic skills' and had 'an excellent educational impact on young viewers during its first year on the air'.

Sesame Street is primarily aimed at teaching school-related skills, such as letters, numbers, forms, relations, classifications and body parts, to disadvantaged 4-year-olds in urban ghettos. In its first year it was estimated that 7 million families viewed the programme and over 250 public and commercial television stations broadcast it.

According to the Malcolm article:

- Disadvantaged children who regularly watch the series show greater gains in learning than advantaged children who watch only infrequently, regardless of age, sex or geographic location.
- Three-year-old regular viewers learn more than four or five-year-old viewers who watch less frequently.
- Children appear to learn equally well watching at home or in pre-school centres, but children who learn the most 'tended

to have mothers who watch the show and discussed it with
them later.'

(quoted in Harvey Lesser *Television's the Preschool Child*,
Academic Press, New York, 1977)

The CTW believe that the major contribution of *Sesame Street* has been to
facilitate the transition from home to school. The programme has been
constantly evaluated and new aspects of the curriculum added. One clear
aspect has been their treatment of disability. By using a positive approach
to the portrayal of disability in *Sesame Street*, the programme has
attempted to remove some of the negative aspects of disability in the
minds of children. By doing this, early stereotyping could be reduced and
acceptance and a supportive attitude be developed towards disability.

In its early days *Sesame Street* was shown twice a day in most areas of the
United States. The audience grew rapidly over the initial year. Widespread
efforts were made to publicise the programme. CTW set up the department
of Community Educational Services. Through this department volunteers
were trained in the techniques of reinforcing the educational objectives of
Sesame Street.

Sesame Street is the most researched educational programme ever
developed. The Educational Testing Services (ETS) of Princeton, New
Jersey was contracted to undertake a major national evaluation. The early
studies showed that there had been significant learning gains in children
both in the middle and lower socioeconomic groups. The research showed
that those who watched more learned more. It became evident that
parental encouragement was a significant factor in learning.

The style of *Sesame Street* is significant. Most educational programmes,
even today are produced by educators whilst other children's programmes
are produced by entertainers. Joan Cooney developed the idea that the best
educational television programmes should be witty, entertaining and fun.
CTW from the outset planned to link the educational research to the
creative writing process. The aim was not just to be a production factory
for children's programmes but to use the research to devise methods of
teaching children effectively. The writers of the series work closely with
the researchers to ensure that their individual goals are achieved. The
approach has had a major impact on the development of children's
television, both in the United States and around the world. Most recent

productions, such as *Teletubbies,* owe much of their philosophy of production to the early ideas developed in the 1960s by CTW.

The early approach of CTW to *Sesame Street* can be summarised as:

■ Establish and use television as a significant tool to address urgent educational priorities.

■ Create a fusion of education with entertainment on a scope unmatched by anything previously attempted in the children's area.

■ Demonstrate the educational cost efficiency of programming which is budgeted, planned and produced well enough to attract a large voluntary audience of home viewers.

■ Devote unprecedented effort to identifying precise educational goals, making extensive participation of expert consultants and advisers a key element.

■ Develop the formative research process, involving pre-broadcast child testing with revisions of the experimental production elements as a central advisory role.

■ Create a management model whereby effective three-way collaboration between researchers, subject specialists and television production specialists runs smoothly.

■ Give special emphasis to the needs of children from low-income families and minority groups.

■ Promote a widespread awareness of television's potential to teach children effectively.

■ Widely demonstrate what is learned in the areas of research, project planning and production.

(Edward Palmer, *Television and America's Children*, Oxford University Press, New York, 1988).

It is this that made the world of CTW and the development of *Sesame Street* unique and explains why the series has achieved the success and longevity which it has achieved.

Sesame Street has developed into 'the longest street in the world'. From a minor studio in Manhattan's Upper West Street, *Sesame Street* has spread to some 89 countries worldwide. The same purposes for which the programme was first produced in the United States are as appropriate for the overseas market as they were for the first US editions. In the words of Gregory Gettas, a producer with CTW International Television Group.

'Children like *Sesame Street*'s humour, tempo, characters, stories and songs. They like its puppets and its fast-paced format. They like its emphasis on audience participation and the sense of mastery it gives them when they learn something new. Here is a programme that speaks to them in their own language, on their level and with respect for their intelligence.'

> Gregory Gettas, The Globalisation of Sesame Street
> in *Educational Technology Research and Development*,
> Vol 38, No 4, 1990

In 1969 CTW set up an international division to licence overseas versions of *Sesame Street*. Four licensing policies were developed:

1 In keeping with the CTW policy that Sesame Street be broadcast commercial free, all foreign versions must also be commercial-free.
2 All changes must meet the highest production standards.
3 All foreign adaptations must be produced to reflect the values and traditions of the host country's culture.
4 All alterations must be approved and supervised by a local committee of educational experts working with CTW.

The first overseas adaptation of *Sesame Street* was in Germany by Norddeutscher Rundfunk (NDR). This was first produced in 1971 as a German dubbed version of the US series. Later, some local segments were included in the programme.

About the same time the Canadian Broadcasting Corporation (CBC) also used *Sesame Street*. A major priority placed by the CBC was a bilingual adaptation – using English and French. Initially five minutes of Canadian material was produced. Today this has been expanded and includes multiculturalism, ecology, native peoples and regional diversity.

Television New Zealand (TVNZ) deleted the Spanish segments of the original US version and inserted in their place live action film and animated sequences dealing with the heritage of the native Maori population.

In 1972 Mexico decided that *Sesame Street* would be extensively redeveloped for their market. Half of the programme would be from the

US version dubbed into Spanish. The remaining half would be a local production including animation, live action films and studio sequences. By developing a board to oversee the production from a wider range of Latin American countries speaking Spanish, the programme could be broadcast throughout Central and South America. *Plaza Sesamo* was thus developed and started broadcasting, in 1973. It still runs in eight Latin American countries.

Twelve other local language series of *Sesame Street* have been produced worldwide. They include:

Vila Sesamo – Brazil
Sesamstraat – Holland and Belgium
Iftah Ya Simsim – Kuwait (16 Arab countries)
Rechov Sumsum – Israel
Rua Sesamo – Portugal (plus Angola and Mozambique)
Susam Sokagi – Turkey
Sesam Stasjon – Norway

A typical co-production consists of 130 half-hour episodes. Approximately half the material is produced locally. All the local products vary – sets differ, writing approaches differ, characters differ and animation techniques differ. Curriculum goals are formatted in different ways and for different purposes in different countries.

Conclusion

The purpose of this case study has been to explain some of the philosophy behind the development of what is clearly the world's most successful educational children's programme. From its roots in the United States in the 1960s, it has spread worldwide. Its approach has been adopted into the way that many children's programmes are made throughout the world. The work of CTW is as relevant today as it was when the initial concepts were developed.

In the words of Keith Mielke, Vice President for Research for the CTW:

CTW has pioneered not only the combination of serious entertainment and serious education via mass media, but also the management processes by which these complex projects were developed. Research and development has been integral to these processes from the very beginning and will be in the future as CTW adapts to a rapidly changing media and social environments.

9 | PRACTICAL WORK

Why undertake practical work?

Some media studies courses are only theoretically based. However, it is our belief that some practical work in media is of equal importance. It is often the case that by being involved in practical media production a deeper understanding of the theoretical concepts will be obtained. When making your first video production you may gain an insight that allows you to view television in a totally different light – maybe appreciating for the first time the way that the programme-makers have constructed their media texts. The concepts already dealt with in this book: ideology, language, narrative, representation, audience and technology, all have a part to play in the making of the video. The process of media production can be a way of more clearly understanding the theoretical concepts behind media studies.

Media production, like all media analysis, is based on the following signpost questions:

MEDIA AGENCIES	– *who* is communicating and why?
MEDIA CATEGORIES	– *what* type of text is it?
MEDIA TECHNOLOGY	– *how* is it produced?
MEDIA LANGUAGE	– *how* do we know what it means?
MEDIA AUDIENCE	– *who* receives it and what sense do they make of it?
MEDIA REPRESENTATION	– *how* does it *present* its subject?

BFI, *Primary Media Education*, 1989

Many aspects of media production involve access to a quantity of technology and also involve working with other people. In video production a team effort is usually required, and of course, access to video equipment. One of the major problems experienced with people making their first productions is that they are too ambitious in their projects – trying to make sophisticated programmes which require access to a wider range of expensive equipment (e.g. in video there are limitations to what you can achieve without an edit suite). Remember also that the video camera you are using probably cost several hundred pounds or dollars. You cannot hope to match the technical quality of broadcast television, but by learning the right techniques you can produce programmes where your audience will watch the content and not concentrate on poor technical understanding.

Various techniques in media production must be learnt to achieve success. Pictures that are out of focus, or difficult to see because they are badly framed or have incorrect exposure will not impress your audience. Remember that your audience are sophisticated media 'readers' – they are used to seeing a wide variety of quality media texts and will, to some extent, view your attempts alongside the texts they are experiencing every day. By learning the correct techniques of production you should aim not to copy those of the media professionals but to make productions which show that you have fully understood the processes of the construction of media texts. Make productions to the highest standards that time, technology and your experience allow, but remember that it is the process rather than the product that is important at this stage. In professional media production it is rare for a product to be fully satisfactory to all involved – there is always room for improvement! However, it is a learning curve; by reflecting on how you went about the practical exercise and by evaluating the product constructively and critically, the experience will prove of value and you will learn to improve.

Photography

Photography is one of the most accessible of all the media technologies. Cameras are available to suit all budgets, from the disposable compacts through sophisticated single lens reflex to full professional cameras – the choice can be quite bewildering!

Cameras

Disposables

The camera contains the film and the camera is sent back to the laboratory for processing. Interesting types include: wide angle which takes two pictures simultaneously and gives a 'panoramic' view; those with built-in flash; and the 'weather-proof' type which can be used at the beach and even in shallow water. It is easy to dismiss these but excellent results can be obtained in some circumstances.

'Polaroid' instant

These have been available for a long time and the most recent cameras are of high quality. Clearly the advantage is that within a couple of minutes of taking the photo you have the results. However, one disadvantage is the cost of each image, which is considerably higher than standard developing and processing. Another disadvantage is that the chemicals impregnated into the prints are unpleasant and potentially hazardous.

Compacts

These are by far the most common cameras in use, ranging in price from an inexpensive basic model with a fixed lens up to very high quality cameras with zoom lenses. Exposure and focus is usually controlled by the camera. Results are usually predictable and the quality can be excellent. However, there are several disadvantages. These are viewfinder cameras – you look through the viewfinder rather than the lens so that framing is not fully predictable. In addition the automatic focus and exposure cannot easily be fooled – the camera always focuses on the closest object, and this can lead to problems. The biggest disadvantage is in the fact that many compacts have fixed wide angle lenses, so often the subject matter is too distant from the camera, making a small, insignificant image in the resulting photograph.

Single lens reflex (SLR)

In an SLR camera, the photographer, via a series of mirrors, looks through the lens when setting up the shot. This makes framing and focusing much easier than with all the above types of camera. SLRs come in a wide range of prices. Features vary from cameras which work in almost completely automatic mode with auto-focus and auto-exposure, through models where the automatic feature may be selected to choose priority in shutter or aperture, to those that are completely manual. Photography students should use manual SLRs so that they can learn to control the camera and to utilise the different focus effects in depth of field, and the effects of using different shutter speeds. Many photographers use a camera in automatic mode most of the time, concentrating on composition and leaving the camera to control most of the functions.

Medium format

These are the cameras frequently used by professional photographers. The larger size of film results in a better quality photograph. However, the cost of the equipment is high and the camera is usually larger and less manageable than SLRs.

Digital

Digital cameras do away with the need for film by using a computer disc. Once the photograph has been taken, the shots can be viewed on a computer and with relevant programs can be manipulated in a variety of ways. Images can be stored on a CD ROM for quick indexing. A wider variety of cameras is now available and prices are progressively dropping. It will probably take a long time for this technology to replace film and photographic prints for many people. However, the future of photography may lie in a digital format.

Film

The basic choice available is:

- black-and-white print film
- colour print film
- reversal film for colour slides.

Colour print film is the most commonly used today. It is generally cheaper and processing is widely available from one-hour to overnight processing at an economic price.

Black-and-white film can be processed commercially but often takes longer and is considerably more expensive than colour film. Many educational establishments and arts centres have darkrooms available where black-and-white films can be processed and printed by the photographer. This gives the photographer control over the final product and allows exploration of the medium of black and white, giving a potentially greater degree of creativity.

Slide film is also an interesting medium. Because there is no negative, the quality of the image is usually higher, but may require a projector to show the transparencies, especially for larger group displays. Reversal film is generally more expensive than colour print film.

The range of makes of film available is wide. Photographers tend to have a personal preference for particular makes of film, and each make of film has some colour cast which can be noticeable. However, the technology of film production has improved to the point where it is difficult to choose between film makes.

There is a wide choice of film speed – i.e. the rate at which the film reacts to light. Generally the 'slower' the film the better the quality of the image. Film speed is measured by the ISO number (International Standard Organisation). The lower the number the slower the film, which requires more light to produce a correctly exposed photograph. In colour print film the most common speeds are ISO 100, 200 and 400; in black and white 125 and 400. For general use 100 and 200 film speeds are useful out of doors in good light situations, while 400 gives greater flexibility in lower light both in and outdoors. In special circumstances where you are working in low light (e.g. where you want to take photographs of a drama production without using flash), fast film of 1000, 1600 or even faster can be used but at the cost of quality.

Camera controls

The camera in manual mode requires you to operate:

- focus
- aperture
- shutter speed.

Once you have chosen a film speed, to obtain a correctly exposed negative you must make sure that sufficient light falls on the film. Aperture controls the amount of light which is allowed through the camera lens. It is measured in f-stops. At the highest number on the aperture ring, often f.22, the least light will travel through the lens. At the lowest aperture, usually f.2.8, the most light will pass through. The importance of these settings is the effect it has on focus. At f.22 most aspects of the image are in focus, while at f.2.8 focus is specific. If you wanted to take a picture of a flower with the foreground and background out of focus you would need a small f-number, while to take a photograph of a large group of people or a landscape f.22 would be more appropriate. This concept is called 'depth of field' and is an important aspect of taking photographs.

Control of shutter speed is also significant. At high shutter speeds of 1/500 or 1/1000 second the action is frozen. Therefore, when taking a picture of a car moving fast, both the car and the background are frozen with no impression of movement. At slow shutter speeds, 1/15 or 1/30 second, the car will show movement against the background with some blurring of the car. By 'panning' – i.e. moving the camera sideways to follow the car while focusing on the car, the car will be perfectly sharp but the background will show movement by being blurred.

Therefore, by choosing different shutter speeds or apertures you can achieve different effects using a manual camera. Clearly, whichever you choose, the correct metering in the camera will be required so that the exposure of the film to light is correct. SLR cameras usually use 'through the lens' metering (TTL) with either lights or needles inside the camera giving an indication of correct exposure.

SLR cameras also have the benefit of allowing you to change lenses. A wide angle lens (typically 28 mm) allows you to take pictures of whole buildings or landscapes from a short distance. The standard lens is the 50 mm, a good general-purpose lens. For portrait photography a short telephoto lens of around 100 mm is best because it allows you to be further away from the subject therefore less intrusive. A longer telephoto lens, from 135 mm to 500 mm plus, can be useful for bringing distant subjects close when you cannot get physically nearer to them.

A further important area in which to experiment is with the use of filters. Some distort the image (e.g. starburst), some reduce reflections (polarising) and others change or enhance colours.

'The camera never lies' is a well-known saying. However all photographs are a distortion of the truth in that they are 'constructed' images. The photographer selects that part of the image he or she wishes to show and by choosing to use different films, lenses, shutter speeds or apertures produces different effects.

I would encourage you to experiment with photography. Try to record how you take each photograph and examine how your experimentation affected the final image.

There is a major difference between snaps and photographs. A *photograph* involves your thinking about the image you are taking for that split second before you actually take it. Whichever camera you use, take time to really look through the viewfinder before pressing the shutter release.

Video

Video has, like photography, become a more accessible technology over recent years as prices of equipment have fallen. The complication is the increasing number of non-compatible formats available.

- **VHS**   Full-size tape machines are available which make the camcorders large. VHS is the lowest quality, the most common in use and the format used in most people's homes.

- **VHSC** is a compact version of the above meaning that the camcorders can also be small. The tapes can be put into an adapter cassette for playing on a full-size machine.

- **SVHS**   A much higher quality than standard VHS. Tapes are approximately twice the price of standard VHS tapes and cannot be played on standard machines. Similarly, both a full-size version and a compact version are available with the advantages and disadvantages as above.

- **Video 8**   Higher quality than VHS and comparable to SVHS. The tapes are small so that the camcorders can also be small. However, Video 8 did not really catch on as a consumer format to replace VHS at home. A semi-professional format is available as **Hi-8**. Camcorders range in price from cheaper domestic models to professional versions costing several thousand pounds or dollars. Some broadcast stations use them for news gathering. However, they are increasingly being replaced by digital formats.

- **Digital**   Three main formats are available: **DV**, **DVCAM** and **DVPRO**. These three formats have some compatibility: DV and DVCAM are similar in the technical way they compress the signal digitally, but DVPRO uses a different system. The digital systems are superior in quality to all the above and will eventually replace them, although VHS will probably take a long time to disappear. The price of digital camcorders varies dramatically depending on whether they are aimed at the domestic user or the professional. DV is the consumer version while DVCAM and DVPRO are designed with the professional user in mind. For example, ITN and CNN have decided to use DVPRO as their major news-gathering format. The battle between DVCAM (Sony) and DVPRO (Panasonic) is interesting and ultimately one will win the acceptance of the market at the expense of the other.

The television industry currently stores material on some 22 formats of tape, although many are old formats. The list includes:

- one-inch reel-to-reel
- U Matic (three types)
- VHS, SVHS, Digital S
- 8mm and Hi8
- Betacam, Betacam SP, Digi Betacam
- D1, D2, D3, D5
- DV, DVCAM, DVPRO, DVCPRO50.

Inevitably there must be a reduction in the formats available and as with still photography where the film will be replaced by a disk, the same will happen in video, with tape being replaced by a digital disk.

The features of video cameras vary considerably.The more expensive professional cameras differ from domestic cameras largely in the quality (and price) of the lens. Cameras such as the Betacam have a smaller range of features compared with the majority of domestic cameras. For example, there is no automatic focus, no auto white balance (the feature which compensates for different light conditions such as television lights, indoor fluorescent lights and natural outdoor lighting), no titling devices, and often no auto iris (to control the light). The viewfinders also vary greatly: some have colour screens, some have large screens on the back of the camera, etc.

Larger cameras can be rested on the shoulder for stability when hand holding, but most amateurs and students will use much smaller cameras.

Using video cameras

The problem you face in making your own programmes is that your audience is sophisticated and used to watching quality broadcast television. Although viewers may not be aware of the actual techniques involved, they know when it looks wrong. Clearly, material you shoot will be compared with the way 'professional' camera operators construct their pictures. Although you cannot match the technical quality of a camera costing many thousands of pounds or dollars with your much less expensive camcorder, you can learn some of the basic lessons and avoid the obvious pitfalls.

Below are ten tips to making better videos.

1 **Autofocus**   Autofocus is useful in some circumstances but the camera is easily confused by what you want to focus on. If you move from one person in the foreground to another the camera will refocus on the background. Most cameras have a switch to enable you to use auto or manual focus – try it and you may find that you get better results by manual focusing.

2 **Framing**   Television is a close-up medium – most television you view uses close-up pictures of people and objects. Most people when first using a camera shoot too far away from the subject. You need, for example, to get detail of eyes and faces in people. A picture known in the jargon as 'medium close-up' (a line drawn at elbow height to the top of the head) is used in television. Another common fault is the amount of room left above the head – known as 'head room'. This should be a small gap in most cases, particularly when you are close. As the eyes are the most important feature of the face, they should be positioned in the most important part of the screen, about one-third of the way down the screen.

3 **Zooming**   In broadcast television the zoom is rarely used. In the words of one expert 'one zoom can be eye catching, more than one zoom an eyesore'. Do not over use the zoom – use it to set up the shot when you are planning the shot on pause, but use it sparingly when recording. A video camera should be thought of as a still camera capable of recording movement. Let the action happen within the frame. You cannot make a picture interesting with lots of zooming.

4 **Panning**   Panning is the sideways movement of the camera. If you continuously move the camera it becomes distracting for the viewer. Follow action with a pan but, like zooming, movement of the camera does not make for interesting pictures.

5 **Use a tripod** Although some cameras now have an anti-shake device built in, this does not overcome the need to use a tripod in many circumstances. Unless circumstances dictate hand-held – for example, very fast action or the camera operator having to move a great deal, use a tripod to get stable pictures. Try to use a tripod with long stable legs and a fluid action head to get smooth movements.

6 **Sound** All camcorders come with a built-in microphone. However, if the sound you are recording is more than a few metres away, the sound quality you obtain will be poor. Most microphones work best at a distance of less than one metre. If you are recording sound further away than this use an additional microphone to get close. By plugging it into your camera you disconnect the in-built microphone. However, with microphones you get the quality you pay for – the very cheapest will give only relatively poor quality. Always, if your camera allows, monitor the sound through headphones – sound lets down more filming than anything else. Be aware of what you are recording.

7 **Lighting** Modern video cameras work extremely well in very low light. However, there are many times when you need to use additional light sources. Television is a two-dimensional image and, when you are showing people and objects, you are trying to show depth – i.e. a three-dimensional image. Watch a television newsreader and notice how the light effects create depth. The principal effect is obtained by lighting the subject from one side at an angle of 45° downwards. This is called key lighting. If necessary there should be a less powerful light from the other side to 'fill' some of the shadows, and a light from the rear to highlight the subject's hair and shoulders to give an increased sense of depth.

Experiment with lighting to see the results – it is worthwhile.

8 **Pre-production planning** One of the major differences between the amateur use of the video camera and the serious film maker is in the process before production takes place. Pre-production planning involves decision making about aspects of the production which will affect the final product.

These include:

a) *audience* – a programme made for the family will be different from one produced for the local video club. Think about what the viewer expects from the video in terms of style and content.

b) *the purpose of the programme* – what do you want the audience to feel or know about after viewing the programme? If you cannot define this then how do you expect the audience to know how to react?

c) *storyboard* – one of the major problems of video production is that it is a visual medium. When you start to plan it is normal to write a script – but what you must do is to visualise what the shots will look like. A storyboard is therefore an important step. Hours of time can be saved by the production of a storyboard. An example of a storyboard format is produced opposite.

d) *decisions on locations and interviewing subjects* – it is important to try to foresee any problems in advance. For example if you need power check whether there is a suitable socket available and any difficulties with sound, such as carrying out a major interview outside on the flight path of a local airport!

9 **Out on the shoot**   Before you start shooting think about the shot you are trying to create.

a) *Direct your shots carefully*, and whenever possible have some action in the shot. Talking heads and general long shots can be very boring and you cannot make them interesting with excessive zooming and panning. You must also realise that shooting an event in real time can be excessively boring when shown to the audience. Would you really wait for a kettle to boil if you were making a programme on how to make a cup of tea?

b) *Continuity* is important, for example actors/presenters must retain the same clothing and hair styles and use the same props in the various takes you make, maybe over several days or even several weeks! You can easily miss something when editing, but when the programme is shown to the audience it will be very noticeable.

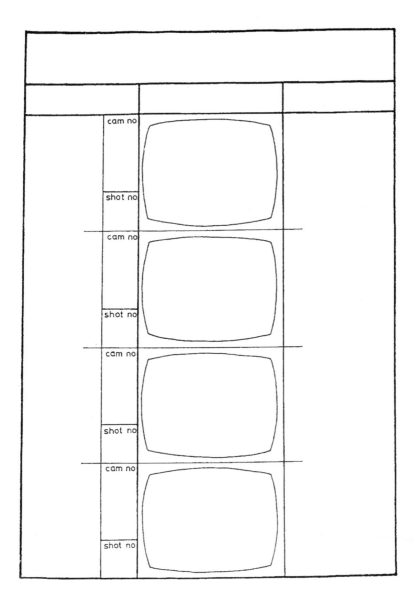

An example of a storyboard format

c) *Always shoot more material than you expect to use* in the final version. It is extremely frustrating to find that you have missed the vital linking shot. In particular, if you have recorded interview material with 'talking heads', i.e. someone standing or sitting in a close-up shot, you will need 'cutaway' material to illustrate what they are talking about. You cannot hold a picture of someone just talking for too long – it becomes very boring for the viewer.

d) *Planning at the time of shooting is critical.* If you have produced a detailed storyboard it makes planning the shoot much easier. Plan your shooting so that it is in a logical order – you do not have to shoot in the same order that the shots will appear on screen if you are going to edit. It is also worthwhile maintaining a detailed shooting log. Record the counter number of the shot, the detail of what you have recorded and note any factors such as whether this is a first or second take of the same event. It is worth using an indicator board to identify each shot at the start.

e) *Always allow a run up time of a least ten seconds when shooting* – you will need this for editing.

10 **Post production** The key is to keep it simple. Video production always takes much longer than you realise at each stage, including post production. In shot selection it is important to keep the individual shots short to maintain interest. A shooting log helps considerably at the start of editing. However, you must log all the material in detail. View all the tapes you have shot and identify all the material, making notes as to the content, both visual and sound. If your camera has timecode (a unique number generated by the camera counting hours, minutes, seconds and frames) this is an easy way of recording the log – if not, use a machine which keeps accurate time in minutes and hours.

For detailed interviews I usually transcribe the content on to paper – including all the 'ums' and 'ers', etc. This is an extremely time-consuming and boring exercise but it is much easier in the long run. From a hard copy you can really sort out what the interviewee has said and identify those parts you want to use. The transcribed scripts should be annotated with the useful parts.

THE PRODUCTION PROCESS FOR A VIDEO DOCUMENTARY

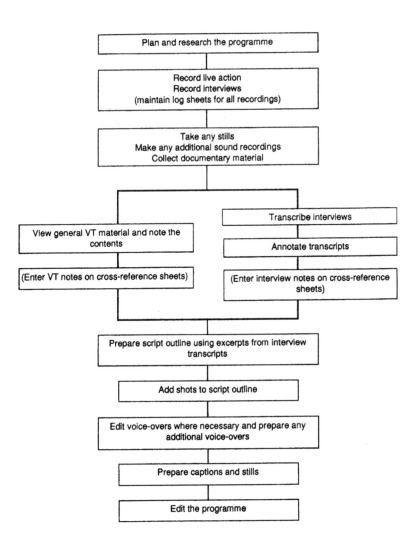

Plan and research the programme

Record live action
Record interviews
(maintain log sheets for all recordings)

Take any stills
Make any additional sound recordings
Collect documentary material

Transcribe interviews

View general VT material and note the contents

Annotate transcripts

(Enter VT notes on cross-reference sheets)

(Enter interview notes on cross-reference sheets)

Prepare script outline using excerpts from interview transcripts

Add shots to script outline

Edit voice-overs where necessary and prepare any additional voice-overs

Prepare captions and stills

Edit the programme

The best way to proceed now is to bring together your log and the transcript to produce a script outline in the form of a paper edit. Write a word script (using the interview as necessary) and identify with it the pictures you want to use. Prepare any captions and identify any stills you want to use. The programme is then ready to edit.

The weakest link in students' programmes, especially documentaries, is usually sound. Although the picture is the dominant medium, sound, if poor, will affect the programme. If, for example, you are mixing sound and voice, set the balance carefully. Background sounds can be extremely distracting if they drown out the voice. If you have recorded poor sound in your shooting, try to overcome this by using a voice-over.

Practical projects

1 A 'promo' film of your school, video club or other relevant organisation to which you belong. Keep it short – say five minutes.

2 A 'travel' film of your locality for a target audience of visiting tourists or businessmen.

3 Documentaries – subject matter can vary enormously, for example, transport problems, conservation, youth facilities locally, etc.

4 Myths and legends – local myths and legends including local castles, haunted buildings, etc.

5 Local news – follow the format of your local television news broadcasts.

Audio

Audio work has the considerable advantage over video production in that the equipment involved is relatively inexpensive. It can also be undertaken by individuals whereas video is really a team operation. However, to be acceptable the quality of the recording is important in audio work – perhaps more so than the quality in video production.

Like photography and video, there is a range of formats available. These include:

■ **Reel-to-reel tape**   This is still often used in professional recording because of the quality and ease of editing. Recorders were first introduced in the 1950s. Domestic versions were used in the 1960s and 1970s but have largely disappeared. Reel-to-reel portable recorders, in particular the Uher, have been used in radio stations but are being progressively replaced by digital systems.

■ **Compact cassettes**   One of the miracles of standardisation in the audio visual world was the adoption of the compact cassette format introduced by Philips in the 1960s. Initially, cassette recorders were low quality but technology has improved so that good quality recording and playback are now available. Professional portable machines are frequently used in interview situations. A micro version of the compact cassette is available and is widely used in dictation machines.

■ **Digital Audio Tape (DAT)**   DAT was introduced in the 1980s as a new tape format which records sound digitally and at much higher quality. Machines have dropped in price and are widely used in professional settings because of the quality that can be achieved. In radio stations DAT tape is edited in a way very similar to videotape. DAT has not been accepted as a domestic format chiefly because record companies did not release albums on this format.

When choosing equipment there are various features to look for. Many cheap recorders come with an internal microphone which is fine for low-quality voice recording but ideally you need to use an external microphone, so ensure that the machine has the appropriate socket. Internal microphones frequently suffer from problems of motor noise from the workings of the recorder and often they are low quality. The sound will be 'muffled' or the pick-up will be general, picking up a lot of background sound as well as the particular voice or sound you want.

An external microphone, even a cheap one, will improve the quality of the recording. Bear in mind that most microphones work best at a distance of some 30 to 50 cm (12 to 18 inches) from the sound source.

Many recorders come with only an automatic recording level. This has advantages in that you cannot over-record the signal, which would lead to distortion. However, the disadvantage is that the signal is 'compressed' – boosting quiet passages and limiting loud passages. This creates 'hiss' on the tape. It is better to have a machine which also has manual recording level control so that you can adjust the recording level.

It is useful if the recorder has a headphone or earphone socket. In all audio work it is important to be able to monitor the sound. You need to be able to check the quality of sound but also it is important to ensure that you do not record any unwanted sound.

Some machines also have noise-reduction systems such as the Dolby systems. These reduce the amount of hiss.

Audio recording

It is important to obtain the best-quality recording possible. Quality to some extent will be limited by the quality of your equipment, in particular the microphones, but the techniques you use will also have a major effect on the recording.

Part of the quality will depend upon the 'acoustics' of the room you are using. A room that has hard surfaces and few items to soak up the sound like curtains, soft furniture and carpet, will mean that there will be a great deal of reflected sound. Sound will be bounced back off the hard surfaces and so you will record direct and indirect sound. If you record in a bathroom the sound will be reflected and you will get an echo effect. Large buildings such as sports halls and churches also suffer from poor acoustics and some have echoes lasting several seconds. If you have to record in these circumstances it is important to get the microphone close to the source of the sound.

Microphones have an optimum distance at which they work best. In most cases this is about 30 cm (12 inches). There are a few specialised microphones used by singers on a stage that allow you to speak or sing right up to the microphone but in most cases if you do this you will just distort the sound.

It is rare to find a recording place which is completely silent. Inside buildings you may find noise from air-conditioning and heating units, humming fluorescent lights, humming electrics from fridges and freezers, etc. Always use your headphones to monitor the sound and cut out any unwanted sound.

When using a microphone be careful of picking up excess noise from it. Rough handling will be picked up from the microphone case as will noise caused by air movement. If you use a microphone stand be careful because vibrations through the floor or table can easily be picked up. If you are using a recorder with a built-in microphone be careful about putting it on a hard surface (e.g. a table) because the motor sound of the machine can easily transfer to the microphone.

Finally, always do a voice test before you start to record. If you have manual recording level, set this to the level of the speaker. Check the test recording by playing it back to check the quality and to ensure there is no background noise. When you start to record them, most people are nervous and will make mistakes at first. Also be aware of the dangers when a person you are recording is reading a script. If the reader rustles the script the noise will be audible on your recording. It is best to lay scripts out side by side so that pages do not have to be turned, or even print them on thin cardboard which does not rustle. Try to give confidence to a reader – do not get irritated when they make mistakes. Even the most professional voice-over artists make mistakes – and often when they have fluffed one piece in a script they will do it again at the same place!

If you have access to a mixer you can make up much more elaborate audiotapes. Mixers are a simple way of laying various tracks together or 'live' mixing sound at the time. Some mixers have recording equipment built into them.

The 'portastudio' can develop elaborate recordings by allowing you to multi-track, i.e. build-up a final recording independently. This is how professionals record music, where each part of the music is recorded separately and then finally mixed down together. A six-channel 'portastudio' allows ten recorded parts to be mixed together by continually remixing. A 'portastudio' is available from a few hundred pounds or dollars upwards depending on its degree of sophistication.

Other simple inexpensive mixers can be obtained, and there are models ranging from a few hundred to many thousands of pounds or dollars for full professional machines. By having two recorders and access to an audio system with cassette or CD, music, sound effects and voice can be mixed together.

Practical projects

1 Copy the output of a radio station. You can record an item for a local news bulletin. Use local newspapers as a source of local news and build up an item using interviews and a newsreader. This can be developed into a radio station using music, station identification tapes, etc.

2 Produce a radio drama. It could be a story that you have written for yourself or an adaption from a book. You can add to the story by the use of sound effects either from CDs or from live effects, and music can be used to enhance atmosphere.

Computers

Print-based material is still a critical part of the media which influence our everyday life. As computers become cheaper and more powerful, the potential to use them to make elaborate designs becomes more available to the ordinary user.

Desk Top Publishing (DTP) packages of software are now cheap and will give you the flexibility to produce newsletters and magazines which are attractive to look at. If your computer does not have DTP then the standard word processing package can be used but you will end up having to 'cut and paste' to design materials.

The graphics packages now available allow you to design on the computer but also frequently to import images from elsewhere. This may be a simple 'clip art' package to allow ready-drawn images to be included. Access to a scanner and/or digitiser will allow images from photographs, video camera or other print images to be included in your material. Again, the price of this hardware is falling and it is becoming more available.

Both hardware and the software packages are being updated so quickly that a detailed description seems rather pointless; by the time this book is published they will be out of date.

Practical project

Produce layouts for newspapers and magazines. The key to successful print material is that it is must be appropriate to the audience. Examine magazines currently available. Consider the style that they use, in particular the graphic design (how pictures, layout and type fonts are used), language and content and how they appeal to the audience, to help you to make decisions on how you want to design your own.

Multimedia is a more sophisticated medium. With the programs which are now becoming available, text and images, both still and moving, and audio can be produced on the computer and recorded on CD ROM. Again the hardware and software is changing so rapidly that today's technology will seem like museum pieces in a short time. However, multimedia will provide a powerful tool for designing material and may in the future change much of the previous technology. There will be a way of constructing still photography, video, audio and DTP work into one medium. However, many of the processes previously described will still be appropriate in multimedia.

Practical work is an important aspect of Media Studies – a way of gaining insights into the processes that operate in the media. In your study practical work should not be an end in itself, but an important route to understanding the theoretical aspects. However, most people also find it very enjoyable!

GLOSSARY

There are several useful books which offer clear explanations of terms used frequently in Media Studies.

ABC of Communication Studies, D Gill and B Adams (Nelson, 1992)

Key Concepts in Cinema Studies, Susan Hayward (Routledge, 1996)

A Dictionary of Narratology, Gerald Prince (Scolar Press, 1987)

Keywords, Raymond Williams (Flamingo, 1981)

anchor   words used to fix a meaning to an image

code   a system of meaning understood by members of the same culture

connotation   meaning added by the audience to what is actually seen in an image

deconstruction   the analysis of a media text by considering each of the separate parts which make up the text

denotation   what is actually shown within an image

diegetic   sound from people or objects onscreen. Other sounds for which we cannot see the sources are said to be non-diegetic.

genre   a type or category of text (e.g. thriller, western)

hegemony   when groups combine to make the power of the dominant group appear natural and legitimate

ideology   a system of ideas

mise en scène   literally the setting up of the place in which the action of a film takes place

montage   consecutive editing together of shots which do not have an obvious link

narrative   a story

plot   the order in which the main events of a story are presented to the audience

representation   how a person, place or thing is portrayed in a media text

semiology   the study of signs

sequence   an ordered series of images

FURTHER READING

Introduction

M Alvarado, R Gutch and T Wollen, *Learning the Media*, Macmillan, 1987
G Burton, *More than Meets the Eye*, Arnold, 1990
M Clarke, *Teaching Popular Television*, Heinemann, 1987
B Dutton, *Media Studies: An Introduction*, Longman, 1995
The English and Media Centre, *Production Practices*, EMC, 1994
J Fiske, *Introduction to Communication Studies*, Methuen, 1982
D Fleming, *Media Teaching*, Blackwell, 1995
S and W Hackman, *Television Studies*, Hodder & Stoughton, 1988
A Hart, *Understanding the Media*, Routledge, 1991
D Lusted (ed.), *The Media Studies Book*, Routledge, 1991
M Mcluhan, *Understanding Media*, Routledge & Kegan Paul, 1964
D McQuail, *Towards a Sociology of Mass Communications*, Collier-MacMillon, 1969
L Masterman, *Teaching about Television*, Macmillan, 1980
L Masterman, *Teaching the Media*, Routledge, 1985
F D Rusmore, *The Purposes of Education*, Institute of Cultural Research, 1974
T O'Sullivan, B Dutton and P Rayner, *Studying the Media*, Arnold, 1994
S Price, *Media Studies*, Pitman, 1993

Dictionaries of terms

BKSTS, *Dictionary of Audio-Visual Terms*, Focal Press, 1983
D Gill and B Adams, *ABC of Communication Studies*, Nelson 1992
P Jarvis, *Teletalk: A Dictionary of Broadcast Terms*, BBC TV Training, 1991
S St Maur, *The A–Z of Video and Audio-Visual Jargon*, Routledge, 1986
J Watson and A Hill, *A Dictionary of Communication & Media Studies*, Edward Arnold, 1993
R Williams, *Keywords – A Vocabulary of Culture and Society*, Fontana Press, 1988

Agencies, ideology and institutions

R C Allen (ed.) *Channels of Discourse*, Methuen, 1987

M Alvarado and J O Thompson (eds) *The Media Reader*, BFI, 1990

M Barker, *Achou: The Story of a Violent Comic*, Titan Books, 1990

C Barr (ed.), *All our Yesterdays*, BFI, 1986

P Cook, *The Cinema Book*, BFI, 1985

A Crisell, *Understanding Radio*, Methuen, 1986

J Curran and J Seaton, *Power without Responsibility: The Press and Broadcasting*, Methuen, 1985

T Dewe Matthews, *Censored*, Chatto and Windus, 1994

T Eagleton, *Ideology*, Verso, 1991

J Eldridge (ed.), *Getting the Message: News, Truth and Power*, Routledge, 1993

L Ferrari and C James, *Wham Wrapping*, BFI, 1990

A Hart, *Teaching Television: The Real World*, Cambridge, 1988

D Jones et al, *Media Hits the Pits*, Campaign for Press and Broadcasting Freedom, 1985

C R Koppes and G D Black, *Hollywood Goes to War*, Macmillan, 1987

F R Leavis and D Thompson, *Culture and Environment*, Chatto & Windus, London, 1933

Minority Press Group, *News Ltd. Why You Can't Read All About It*, Comedia, 1981

MOMI Education Dept., *MOMI The Video and Workbook*, BFI, 1992

G Murdoch and P Golding, 'For a Political Economy of Mass Communications' in R Miliband and J Saville (eds), *The Socialist Register 1973*, Merlin, London, 1974

T Pratchett, *Moving Pictures*, Corgi, 1991

J Shand and T Wellington, *Don't Shoot the Best Boy*, Currency, 1988

J Tunstall, *Television Producers*, Routledge, 1993

G Turner, *Film as Social Practice*, Routledge, 1988

J Twitchin, *Black and White Media Show*, Trentham, 1988

I Wall, *The Industry Pack*, Film Education, 1990

Narrative

D Bordwell and C Thompson, *Film Art: An Introduction*, McGraw Hill, 1997

British Film Institute, *History of Narrative Codes in Film*, BFI Education

British Film Institute/BBC, *Screening Middlemarch*, BFI/BBC, 1994

P Cook, *The Cinema Book*, BFI, 2nd ed. 1990

R Dyer, *Coronation Street*, BFI, 1981

J Fiske, *Television Culture*, Methuen, 1987

B W Kawin, *How Movies Work*, University of California, 1992

D Lusted (ed.), *The Media Studies Book*, Routledge, 1991

B MacMahon and R Quin, *Real Images*, Macmillan, 1986

L Masterman, *Teaching the Media*, Comedia, 1985

J Palmer, *Potboilers*, Routledge, 1991

C Potter, *Image, Sound and Story: The Art of Telling in Film*, Secker and Warburg, 1990

S Price, *Media Studies*, Pitman Publishing, 1993

G Turner, *Film as Social Practice*, Routledge, 1988

Representation

General

M Barker, *Comics, Ideology, Power and the Critics*, Manchester University Press, 1989

J Curran et al (eds), *Bending Reality*, Pluto Press, 1986

J Grahame, *Advertising*, The English and Media Centre, 1994

T O'Sullivan et al, *Studying the Media*, Arnold, 1994

T Perkins, 'Rethinking Stereotypes' in M Barrett et al (eds), *Ideology and Cultural Production*, Croom Helm, 1979

G Swanson 'Representation' in D Lusted (ed.), *The Media Studies Book*, Routledge 1991

Gender

H Baehr and G Dyer (eds), *Boxed In: Women and Television*, Pandora, 1987

H Baehr and A Gray, *Turning it On*, Arnold, 1995

J Berger, *Ways of Seeing*, BBC/Penguin, 1972

G Branston, *Film and Gender*, Film Education, 1994

British Film Institute, *Selling Pictures*, BFI, 1983

M E Brown (ed.), *Television and Women's Culture*, Sage, 1990

S Cook (ed.), *Women and Film Bibliography*, BFI, 1992

K Durkin, *Television, Sex Roles and Children*, Open University Press, 1985

R Dyer, *Star Dossier 1: Marilyn Monroe*, BFI, 1980

R Dyer, *Heavenly Bodies*, Macmillan, 1986

R Dyer, C Geraghty et al, *Coronation Street*, Television Monograph No. 13, BFI, 1981

The English and Media Centre, *Powerful Texts*, EMC, 1994

M Ferguson, *Forever Feminine: Women's Magazines and the Cult of Femininity*, Heinemann, 1983

J Fiske, *Television Culture*, Methuen, 1987

C Geraghty, *Women and Soap Opera*, Polity Press, 1990

E Goffman, *Gender Advertisements*, Macmillan, 1979

J Grahame, *Advertising*, The English and Media Centre, 1994

A Gray, *Video Playtime: The Gendering of a Leisure Technology*, Routledge, 1992

M MacDonald, *Representing Women*, Arnold, 1995

A McRobbie, *Feminimism and Youth Culture: From Jackie to Just Seventeen*, Macmillan, 1991

D Morley, *Family Television*, Comedia/Routledge, 1986

D Morley, *Television, Audiences and Cultural Studies*, Routledge, 1992

V Walkerdine, *Schoolgirl Fictions*, Verso, 1990

A Wernick, *Promotional Culture*, Sage, 1991

J Williamson, *Decoding Advertisements*, Marion Boyars, 1978

J Winship, *Inside Women's Magazines*, Pandora, 1987

L van Zoonen, *Feminist Media Studies*, Sage, 1994

Race

M Anwar, *Television in a Multi-Racial Society*, Commission for Racial Equality, 1982

British Film Insitute, *Black and Asian Catalogue*, BFI, 1995

British Film Institute, *Black Film Video List*, BFI, 1992

P Cohen and C Gardner, *It Ain't Half Racist, Mum*, Comedia, 1982

J Daniels and F Gerson (eds), *The Colour Black*, BFI, 1989

P Hartmann and C Husband, *Racism and the Mass Media*, Davis-Poynter, 1974

J Pines (ed.), *Black and White in Colour*, BFI, 1992

J Twitchen (ed.), *The Black and White Media Show Book: Handbook for the Study of Racism and Television*, Trentham Books, 1988

Genre

British Film Institute, *Film Noir Pack*, BFI

British Film Institute, *Genre Teaching Pack*, BFI

British Film Institute, *Some Visual Motifs of Film Noir*, BFI

British Film Institute, *Western Project*, BFI

I Cameron (ed.), *The Movie Book of Film Noir*, Studio Vista, 1992

M Clarke, *Teaching Popular Television*, Heinemann, 1987

J Fiske, *Television Culture*, Methuen, 1987

J Grahame 'Genre' in J Grahame and N Mayman, *Criminal Records: Teaching TV Crime Series*, BFI, 1988

J Grahame and N Mayman, *Criminal Records*, BFI, 1988

B Grant, *Film Genre Reader*, University of Texas Press, 1986

S Jenkins, *Death of a Gangster*, BFI

B McMahon and R Quin, *Real Images*, Macmillan, 1986

S Neale, *Genre*, BFI, 1980

K Newman, *Nightmare Movies*, Bloomsbury, 1988

K Newman, *Wild West Movies*, Bloomsbury, 1990

D Pirie, *Hammer Horror: A Cinema Case-Study*, BFI, 1988

T Thwaites et al, *Tools for Cultural Studies*, Macmillan, 1994

R Twitchen and J Birkett, *Starters*, BFI, 1983

I Wall, *Genre*, Film Education, 1993

Advertising

J Berger, *Ways of Seeing*, BBC/Penguin, 1972

J Corner, *Television Form and Public Address*, Arnold, 1995

The English and Media Centre, *Powerful Texts*, EMC, 1994

E Goffman, *Gender Advertisements*, Macmillan, 1979

J Grahame, *Advertising* (pack and video), The English and Media Centre, 1994

W Leiss, S Kline and S Jhally, *Social Communication in Advertising*, Methuen, 1986

K Myers, *Understains*, Comedia, 1986

V Packard, *The Hidden Persuaders*, Penguin, 1960

M Schudson, *Advertising, the Uneasy Persuasion*, Routledge, 1992

The Scottish Film Council, *Baxters: The Magic of Advertising*, SFC, 1983

R Shaw (ed.), *The Spread of Sponsorship*, Bloodaxe, 1993

P Stobart (ed.), *Brand Power*, Macmillan, 1994

P Taylor, *Smoke Ring: The Politics of Tobacco*, The Bodley Head, 1984

T Vestergaard and K Schroder, *The Language of Advertising*, Blackwell, 1985

A Wernick, *Promotional Culture*, Sage, 1991

J Williamson, *Decoding Advertisements*, Marion Boyars, 1978

Media – Radio, Popular Music, Newspapers
Radio

S Barnard, *On the Radio: Music Radio in Britain*, Open University Press, 1989

A Crissell, *Understanding Radio*, Methuen, 1986

S Frith, *The Sociology of Rock*, Constable, 1978

C S Higgins and P D Moss, *Sounds Real: Radio in Everyday Life*, University of Queensland Press, 1982

P M Lewis (ed.), *Radio Drama*, Longman, 1981

P M Lewis and J Booth, *The Invisible Medium: Public Commercial and Community Radio*, Macmillan, 1989

The Radio Authority, *Code of Advertising Standards and Practice and Programme Sponsorship*, The Radio Authority

The Radio Authority, *Programme Codes 1 and 2*, The Radio Authority

P Scannell (ed.), *Broadcast Talk*, Sage, 1991

J Tunstall, *The Media in Britain*, Constable, 1983

P Wilby and A Conroy, *The Radio Handbook*, Routledge, 1994

Popular Music

S Barnard, *On the Radio: Music Radio in Britain*, Open University Press, 1989

A Blake, *The Music Business*, Batsford, 1992

I Chambers, *Urban Rythms: Pop Music and Popular Culture*, Macmillan, 1985

F Dannen, *Hit Men: Power Brokers and Fast Money Inside the Music Business*, Vintage, 1991

M Eliot, *Rockonomics: The Money Behind the Music*, Omnibus, 1990

L Evans, *Women, Sex and Rock 'n' Roll*, Pandora, 1994

L Ferrari and C James (eds), *Wham! Wrapping: Teaching the Music Industry*, BFI, 1989

S Frith (ed.), *Facing the Music: Essays on Pop, Rock and Culture*, Mandarin, 1988

S Frith and A Goodwin (eds), *On Record: Rock, Pop and the Written Word*, Routledge, 1990

G Gaar, *She's a Rebel*, Blandford, 1993

N George, *The Death of Rythm and Blues*, Omnibus, 1988

A Goodwin, *Dancing in the Distraction Factory: Music Television and Popular Culture*, Routledge, 1993

S Jones, *Rock Formation: Music, Technology and Mass Communication*, Sage, 1992

L Lewis (ed.), *The Adoring Audience: Fan Culture and Popular Media*, Routledge, 1992

F Lloyd (ed.), *Deconstructing Madonna*, Batsford, 1993

F Malm and R Wallis, *Media Policy and Music Activity*, Routledge, 1992

K Negus, *Producing Pop: Culture and Conflict in the Popular Music Industry*, Arnold, 1992

S Redhead, *The End-of-the-Century Party: Youth and Pop towards 2000*, Manchester University Press, 1990

J Rogan, *Wham! Confidential: The Death of a Supergroup*, Omnibus, 1987

J Rogan, *Starmakers and Svengalis: The History of British Pop Management*, Futura, 1988

S Steward and S Garrett, *Signed, Sealed and Delivered: True Life Stories of Women in Pop*, Pluto, 1984.

Newspapers

Calcutt Report, *Report of the Committee on Privacy and Related Matters*, HMSO, 1990

P Chippendale and C Horrie, *Stick It Up Your Punter: The Rise and Fall of the Sun*, Mandarin, 1990

P Chippendale and C Horrie, *Disaster: The Rise and Fall of the News on Sunday*, Sphere, 1988

M Cockerell, P Hennessy and D Walker, *Sources Close to the Prime Minister*, Macmillan, 1984

S Cohen and J Young (eds.), *The Manufacture of News*, Constable, 1973

J Curran (ed.), *The British Press: A Manifesto*, Macmillan, 1978

J Curran et al (eds.), *Bending Reality*, Pluto, 1986

The English and Media Centre, *Front Page News*, EMC

The English and Media Centre, *Choosing the News*, Teaching exercise, EMC, 1990

R Fowler, *Language in the News: Discourse and Ideology in the Press*, Routledge, 1991

B Franklin and D Murphy, *What News? The Market, Politics and the Local Press*, Routledge, 1991

R Grose, *The Sun-sation: the inside story of Britain's Best-Selling Daily Newspaper*, Angus and Robertson, 1989

R Harris, *Gotcha! The Media, the Government and the Falkands Crisis*, Faber and Faber, 1983

M Hollingsworth, *The Press and Political Dissent*, Pluto Press, 1986

R Keeble, *The Newspapers Handbook*, Routledge, 1994

M Leapman, *Barefaced Cheek: the apotheosis of Rupert Murdoch*, Hodder & Stoughton, 1983

B McNair, *News and Journalism in the UK*, Routledge, 1994

D Morrison and H Tumber, *Journalists at War: the Dynamics of News Reporting During the Falklands Conflict*, Sage, 1988

R Negrine, *Politics and the Mass Media in Britain,* Routledge, 1989

H Porter, *Lies, Damned Lies*, Chatto and Windus, 1984

J Price, *The Newspaper Study Pack*, Macmillan, 1989

P Tatchell, *The Battle for Bermondsey*, Heretic, 1983

J Tunstall, *The Media in Britain*, Constable, 1983

K Waterhouse, *Daily Mirror Style*, Mirror Books, 1981

G Williams, B*ritain's Media: How They are Related,* Campaign for Press and Broadcasting Freedom, 1994

C Wintour, *The Rise and Fall of Fleet Street*, Hutchinson, 1989

Audiences

I Ang, *Desperately Seeking the Audience*, Routledge, 1991

I Ang, *Watching Dallas*, Methuen, 1985

J Blumler and D McQuail, *Television in Politics: its uses and influence*, Faber & Faber, 1968

D Buckingham, *Public Secrets: EastEnders and its Audience*, BFI, 1987

D Buckingham (ed.), *Young People and the Media*, Manchester University Press, 1993

I Chater et al, *Movie Mogul pack*, Film Education, 1994

J Curran et al (eds), *Bending Reality*, Pluto, 1986

J Ellis, *Visible Fictions*, RKP, 1982

J Fiske, *Television Culture*, Methuen, 1987

J Fiske, *Understanding Popular Culture*, Routledge, 1990

J Fowles, *Why Viewers Watch: A Reappraisal of Television Effects*, Sage, 1992

C Geraghty, *Women and Soap Opera: A Study of Prime Time Soaps*, Polity Press, 1991

A Gray, *Video Playtime*, Routledge, 1992

S Hall et al (eds), *Culture, Media and Language*, Hutchinson, London, 1980

A Hart, *Understanding the Media*, Routledge, 1991

D Hebdige, *Subculture: The Meaning of Style*, Methuen, 1979

D Hobson, 'Crossroads': *The Drama of a Soap Opera*, Methuen, 1982

E Katz and P Lazarsfeld, *Personal Influence*, Free Press, Glencoe, Illinois, 1955

P Lazarsfeld, B Berelson and H Gaudet, *The People's Choice*, Duell, New York, Sloane, Pearce, 1944

S Livingstone, *Making Sense of Television*, Butterworth, 1995

S Livingstone and P Lunt, *Talk on Television: Audience Participation and Public Debate*, Routledge, 1994

J Lull, *Inside Family Viewing*, Routledge, 1990

L Masterman, *Teaching the Media*, Routledge, 1985

D McQuail (ed.) *Sociology of Mass Communication*, Penguin, 1972

R Merton, *Mass Persuasion*, Free Press, New York, 1946

M Messenger Davies, *Television Is Good For Your Kids*, Hilary Shipman, 1989

S Moores, *Interpreting Audiences*, Sage, 1993

D Morley, *Family Television*, Comedia, 1986

D Morley, *The Nationwide Audience*, BFI, 1980

D Morley, *Television, Audiences and Cultural Studies*, Routledge, 1992

G Philo, *Seeing and Believing: The Influence of Television*, Routledge, 1990

J Root, *Open the Box*, Comedia, 1986

E Seiter et al, *Remote Control Television, Audiences and Cultural Power*, Routledge, 1989

P Simpson (ed.), *Parents Talking Television*, Comedia, 1987

L Taylor and B Mullan, *Uninvited Guests*, Chatto and Windus, 1986

News

M Alvarado and J O Thompson (eds), *The Media Reader*, BFI, 1990

BBC, *Impartiality: Representing Reality*, BBC, 1989

M Clarke, *Teaching Popular Television* (Chapter 5), Heinemann, 1987

M Cockerell, *Live from Number 10: The Inside Story of Prime Ministers and Television*, Faber, 1988

S Cohen and J Young, *The Manufacture of News*, Constable, 1973, (Revised and extended 1981, especially Part One)

G Cumberbatch et al, *Television and the Miners' Strike*, Broadcasting Research Unit, BFI, 1986

J Curran and J Seaton, *Power without Responsibility: The Press and Broadcasting in Britain*, Routledge, 1988

L Curtis, *Ireland: The Propaganda War*, Pluto, 1984

P Drummond and R Paterson (eds), *Television in Transition*, BFI, 1985

H Evans, *Headline Photography: The Pictures that Made the News*, Treasure Press, 1990

H Evans, *Pictures on a Page: Photojournalism, Graphics and Picture Editing*, Heinemann, 1978

J Fiske, *Television Culture* (Chapter 15), Methuen, 1987

N Garnham, *Capitalism and Communication: Global Culture and the Economics of Information*, Sage, 1990

Glasgow University Media Group, *Really Bad News*, Writers and Readers, 1982

A Goodwin, *Media Studies for Adults*, BFI Education, 1988

M Gurevitch, 'The Globalisation of Electronic Journalism' in J Curran and M Gurevitch (eds), *Mass Media and Society*, Arnold, 1991

S Hall et al, *Policing the Crisis*, Macmillan, 1978

R Harris, *Gotcha! The Media, the Government and the Falklands Crisis*, Faber and Faber, 1983

R Harris, *Good and Faithful Servant*, Faber and Faber, 1990

A Hart, *Understanding the Media* (Chapter 3), Routledge, 1991,

J Hartley, *Understanding News*, Methuen, 1982

M Hollingsworth, *The Press and Political Dissent: A Question of Censorship*, Pluto, 1986

B Ingham, *Kill the Messenger*, Fontana, 1991

N Jones, *Strikes and the Media*, Blackwell, 1986

B McNair, *News and Journalism in the UK: A Text Book*, Routledge, 1994

J Mansfield, *News, News: News Gathering to TV*, BBC TV Training, 1991

L Masterman, *Teaching about Television*, Macmillan, 1980

L Masterman, *Teaching the Media*, Routledge, 1985

L Masterman, 'The Battle of Orgreave' in L Masterman (ed.), *Television Mythologies*, Routledge, 1985

R Negrine, *Politics and the Mass Media in Britain*, Routledge, 1989

G Philo, *Seeing and Believing*, Routledge, 1990

J Root, *Open the Box* (Chapter 4), Comedia, 1986

P Schlesinger, *Putting 'Reality' Together*, Constable, New edition 1987

P Schlesinger, G Murdock and P Elliott, *Televising Terrorism*, Comedia, 1983

P Schlesinger and H Tumber, *Reporting Crime*, OUP, 1994

J Whale, *The Politics of Media*, Fontana, 1977

R Williams, *Raymond Williams on Television: Selected Writings*, Routledge, 1989

Case Study CTW

CTW, *Sesame Street Research Bibliography*, 1990

CTW, *What Research Indicated About The Educational Effect of Sesame Street*, 1991

Educational Technology – Research and Development Journal, Vol 38, No 4, 1990 (edition devoted to CTW)

Lesser, Gerald, *Children and Television – Lessons from Sesame Street*, Random House, 1974

Lesser, Harvey, *Television and the Preschool Child,* Academic Press, New York, 1977

Palmer, Edward L, *Television and America's Children – a Crisis of Neglect*, Oxford University Press, New York, 1988

By accessing databases such as ERIC and DIALOG many of the articles and publications relating to CTW and *Sesame Street* can be obtained.

Practical work

M Alvarado and O Boyd-Barratt (eds), *Media Education: An Introduction* (Section on Practice), BFI, 1992

J Bowker, *Secondary Media Education: A Curriculum Statement*, BFI, 1991

E Boyce et al, *Editing Film and Videotape*, BBC TV Training, 1986

K Chater, *The Television Researcher's Guide*, BBC TV Training, 1989

M Crisp, *After Tea We'll Do The Fight*, BBC TV Training, 1987

G Crofton, *Television Training: Approaches to Production and Directing*, BBC TV Training, 1991

G Crofton, *From Script to Screen*, BBC TV Training, 1986

R Dizazzo, *Corporate Television*, Focal Press, 1990

C Fraser, *The Production Assistant's Survival Guide*, BBC TV Training, 1990

J Grahame, *Production Practices*, English and Media Centre, 1994

J Hedgecoe, *Hedgecoe on Video*, Octopus Publishing, 1989

S Isherwood and N Stanley (eds), *Creating Vision: Photography and the National Curriculum*, Arts Council, 1993

P Jarvis, *Shooting on Location*, BBC TV Training, 1986

S Kruger and I Wall, *Practical Media*, Nelson, 1994

J Mansfield, *Music and Sound Effects: Sound for Television*, BBC TV Training, 1992

G Millerson, *The Technique of Television Production*, Focal Press, 1992

R Montagu, *The Television Graphics Handbook*, BBC TV Training, 1991
B Phillips, *Stand by Studio*, BBC TV Training, 1987
M Rabiger, *Directing the Documentary*, Focal Press, 1992
R Singleton-Turner, *Continuity Notes*, BBC TV Training, 1988
H Snoad, *Directing Situation Comedy*, BBC TV Training, 1988
R Stafford, *Hands On: A Teacher's Guide to Media Technology*, BFI, 1993
A Stamp and G Stone, *The Television Programme*, Sheffield Media Association, 1987
H Watts, *Directing on Camera*, AAVO, 1992
H Watts, *On Camera: How to Produce Film and Video*, BBC, 1984
A Wurtzel, *Television Production*, McGraw Hill, 1985

Magazines (UK)

British Journalism Review, quarterly. c/o John Libbey Media, Faculty of Humanities, University of Luton, Beds LU1 3AJ
Broadcast, weekly trade journal
Campaign, weekly trade journal for advertising
Free Press, journal for the Campaign for Press and Broadcasting Freedom
The Guardian newspaper, Monday edition has a media supplement
The Independent newspaper, Wednesday edition has a media supplement
In The Picture, quarterly. c/o Yorkshire & Humberside Arts, 21 Bond Street, Dewsbury WE13 1AX
The Radio Magazine, weekly
Radio Times, weekly television listings
The Stage & Television Today, weekly journal for television and theatre
Televisual, monthly journal for television production
UK Press Gazette, journalism's weekly newspaper

USEFUL ADDRESSES

United Kingdom

Advertising Standards Authority
2 Torrington Place
London WC1E 7HW
Tel: 0171 580 5555
Supervises advertising to ensure
that it is legal, decent, honest and
truthful.

Arts Council of England
14 Great Peter Street
London SW1P 3NQ
National body to encourage and
support the arts.

British Board of Film
Classification (BBFC)
3 Soho Square
London W1V 6HD
Tel: 0171 439 7961
Classifies film and video.

British Broadcasting Corporation
Broadcasting House
Portland Place
London W1A 1AA
Tel: 0171 580 4468
Corporate headquarters and
location of BBC Radio

British Broadcasting Corporation
Television Centre
Wood Lane
London W12 7RJ
Tel: 0171 743 8000
Location of BBC Television

British Film Institute
21 Stephen Street
London W1P 2LN
Tel: 0171 255 1444
http://www.worldserver.pipex.com./bfi/
Encourages the development of the
art of film. Produces a wide range
of educational material and
publications.

British Sky Broadcasting Ltd
6 Centaurs Business Park
Grant Way
Isleworth TW7 5QD
Tel: 0171 705 3000
Provides Sky channels.

Broadcasters' Audience Research
Board (BARB)
5th Floor, North Wing
Glenthorne House
Hammersmith Grove
London W6 OND
Tel: 0181 741 9110
Produces statistical research on
television audiences.

Broadcasting Standards
Commission
7 The Sanctuary
London SW1P 3JS
Tel: 0171 233 0544
Conducts research and investigates
complaints about broadcast content
(taste and decency, fairness and
invasion of privacy).

Cable Communications
Association
5th Floor
Artillery House
Artillery Row
London SW1P 1RT
Trade association for cable
companies.

Campaign for Press and
Broadcasting Freedom
8 Cynthia Street
London N1 9JF
Tel: 0171 278 4430
Conducts research for more
diverse, accessible and accountable
media.

Channel Four Television
124 Horseferry Road
London SW1P 2TX
Tel: 0171 396 4444
Since 1993 broadcasting Channel 4.

Channel Five Broadcasting
22 Long Acre
London WC2E
Tel: 0171 550 5555
Since 1997 broadcasting Channel 5.

English and Media Centre
136 Chalton Street
London SW1V 4LH
Tel: 0171 828 8560
Resource centre on media
education with useful publications.

Film Education
5th Floor, 41–42 Berners Street
London W1P 3AA
Tel: 0171 637 9932
Film industry sponsored body
producing teaching materials.

Independent Television
Commission (ITC)
33 Foley Street
London W1P 7LB
Tel: 0171 255 3000
Regulates all Independent
Television Services. Produces
useful publications e.g. Codes and
Guidelines. A public access library.

Museum of the Moving Image
South Bank
London SE1 8XT
Tel: 0171 928 3535
Museum telling the story of moving
images from earliest pre-cinema to
television. Excellent bookshop.

National Museum of Photography,
Film & Television
Pictureville
Bradford BD1 1NQ
Tel: 01274 725347
Museum covering all aspects of
the media.

Northern Ireland Film Council
21 Ormeau Avenue
Belfast BT2 8HD
Tel: 01232 232444
Promotes interests of film and
television in Northern Ireland.

Radio Authority
Holbrook House
14 Great Queen Street
London WC2
Tel: 0171 430 2724
Regulates all Independent radio
services.

The Royal Television Society
Holborn Hall
100 Grays Inn Road
London WC1X 8AL
Tel: 0171 430 8000
Society for all those working in or
with an interest in television. Local
groups with meetings and visits.

Scottish Film Council
Dowanhill
74 Victoria Crescent Road
Glasgow G12 9JN
Tel: 0141 334 4445
Promotes all aspects of the
moving-image culture in Scotland.

Skillset
124 Horseferry Road
London SW1P 2TX
Tel: 0171 306 8585
Training organisation for the
broadcast, film and video industries.

Voice of the Listener and Viewer
101 King's Drive
Gravesend
Kent DA12 5BQ
Tel: 01474 352835
A consumer body representing
viewers' and listeners' opinions on
broadcasting issues. Publishes
newsletter and briefings.

Wales Film Council
Screen Centre
Llantrisant Road
Llandaff
Cardiff CF5 2PU
Tel: 01222 578633
Cyngor Ffilm Cymru. Promotes
and develops the culture of the
moving image in Wales.

A comprehensive list of useful
addresses is published in:

British Film Institute, *Film and
Television Yearbook* (annual
publication)

British Television Commission,
Factfile (annual publication).

Australia

Australian Teachers of Media
PO Box 222
Carlton South Victoria 3053
Australia

Rushden Media
Rushden Campus
Deakin University
662 Blackburn Road
Clayton North 3168
Victoria
Australia

Canada

The Centre for Media Literacy
3040 Sherbrooke St West
Room 4B.1
Montreal
QC H3Z 1AA
Canada

Wright Communications
2400 Dundass Street West
Unit 6 Suite 107
Mississaugua
Ontario,
Canada L5K 2RB

New Zealand

Newspapers in Education
The Dominion/Evening Post
PO Box 3740
Wellington
New Zealand

United States of America

Centre for the Study of Communication of Culture
321 N. Spring Avenue
PO Box 56907
St. Louis
MO 63156-0907
USA

Media Workshop
333 W 17th Street
Room 324
New York
NY 10011
USA

INDEX

Page numbers in bold indicate a major reference, those in italic refer to a glossary definition.

Other related titles

 TEACH YOURSELF

POSTMODERNISM

Glenn Ward

One of the most fiercely disputed terms of the late twentieth century, postmodernism has had an impact in most fields, from literature and the visual arts, to cultural studies and sociology. In each of these areas, the meanings of postmodernism are flexible, but in all cases it forces us to question some of our most cherished assumptions. Postmodern debates suggest that our most ingrained ideas about the nature of history, culture, meaning and identity can no longer be taken for granted. As such, it has far-reaching implications for how we think about the world today.

This book is an indispensable guide to this sometimes demanding terrain. Aimed at readers encountering theories of postmodernism for the first time, it places the subject in a wide context. Rather than give an account of the 'postmodern condition' from a single perspective, it offers an introduction to the most important theorists in a number of different disciplines, and links theoretical questions to an eclectic range of examples, from both 'high' and 'popular' culture.

Glenn Ward is a lecturer in the Faculty of Art and Music at Bath College of Art and Design.

Other related titles

TEACH YOURSELF

CULTURAL STUDIES

Will Brooker

Teach Yourself Cultural Studies provides a comprehensive introduction to this popular and exciting subject. The key theorists and issues are discussed in a lively and easy-to-follow style – suitable for both beginners and first-level students.

The book:

- introduces and explains Cultural Studies from its historical origins to recent work on video games, TV fandom and the internet
- summarises, examines and critiques the work of key theorists
- communicates complex ideas in a clear and concise way.

Will Brooker has lectured in Media, Film and Communication Studies and is currently researching and teaching at the University of Wales, Cardiff.